To Hear
the Angels Sing

To Hear the Angels Sing

AN ODYSSEY OF CO-CREATION
WITH THE DEVIC KINGDOM

Dorothy Maclean

Lindisfarne Press

Published by Lindisfarne Press
RR 4, Box 94 A-1
Hudson, NY 12534

ISBN 0-940262-37-1

Library of Congress Cataloging-in-Publication Data

Maclean, Dorothy.
    To hear the angels sing : an odyssey of co-creation with the devic kingdom / Dorothy Maclean.
        p.   cm.
    Reprint. Originally published: Elgin, Ill. : Lorian Press, 1980.
    ISBN 0-940262-37-1 : $10.95
    1. Maclean, Dorothy.   2. Angels —Miscellanea.   3. Nature —Miscellanea.   4. Spirit writings.   5. Occultist —Biography.
6. Findhorn Community —Biography.   7. Lorian Association —Canada —Biography.   I. Title.
BF1408.2.M33A3   1990
133' .092 —dc20
[B]   90-46049
                                                                  CIP

*To all who
aim at enhancing the Divine
in each other and
in all life.*

Contents

Acknowledgements

Acknowledgement and grateful thanks are given for the use of extracts from the following books:

Dictionary of All Scriptures and Myths © 1977 G.A. Gaskell. Reprinted by permission of Crown Publishers Inc.

Unfinished Animal © 1976 Theodore Roszak. Reprinted by permission of Faber & Faber Ltd. and Doubleday & Co. Inc.

Knowing Woman © 1973 Irene Claremont de Castillejo. Reprinted by permission of Hodder & Stoughton Ltd.

The Language of Silence © 1970 Allen Boone. Published by Harper & Row Inc.

Sources edited by Theodore Roszak, published by Harper & Row Inc. © 1972 Theodore Roszak, Edward Hymans, Joseph Epes Brown.

*Man, Know Yourself
and You will Know
the Universe and
the Gods.*

Foreword by David Spangler

In the field of human drama, no stories are quite so gripping nor quite so satisfying and fulfilling in their resolution as tales of separation and subsequent reunion. The quests of lovers, companions, co-workers and families to be reunited after being parted are a mainstay of both fiction and human interest reporting. Particularly when so many people experience aloneness and a sense of separation from some essential or fulfilling part of themselves or of life, such stories appeal as triumphs over alienation and as the restoration of wholeness.

This book tells such a story, save that it is not fiction. It is the account, expressed through the life of a most remarkable woman, of a very real and very important reunion taking place now. To me, it is more exciting than anything of fiction.

Much has been written in recent years about the alienation of our technological culture from nature. The messages of environmental pollution and threats to the eco-sphere, of conflict between conservationists and ecologists on the one hand and industrialists, land developers and energy companies on the other, are so familiar as to become at times only a background noise, joining all the other messages of unrest, decay and disaster that give modern life such a tension of dis-ease.

This book also deals with alienation, but it is not another description of the problem. Instead, it speaks of an answer, of healing this alienation at its source, which is in the realm of our consciousnesses, our attitudes and perspectives, our awarenesses and our world views. It is a book about the creative essences behind natural phenomena and, by contrast, about our creative or spiritual essence as well. It is about the unity, the creative kinship between these essences and ourselves, a unity forgotten by occidental humanity.

It is the forgetting that creates the alienation and all the ills we visit upon our world; it is the remembering that reunites us. Dorothy is a messenger of that memory, a forerunner of a planetary wholeness.

This book is her story of her contact, while at the spiritual community of Findhorn in Scotland and subsequently, after she returned to North America, with these creative essences or living creative principles within nature. She calls them 'devas'. They are the angels that govern the natural order, working joyously, skilfully and wisely with the light of God. As her communications with them point out, humanity too is a deva, a creative being of light. Both these species, one physical and the other existing in an invisible dimension of pure thought and energy, create the forms of the world through which spirit may reveal itself. When this creation takes place in obliviousness (on our part) of this other kingdom of life and even at times in opposition to its purposes, which are for the benefit of all things, not only human beings—in short, when we act chauvinistically toward our world—then we disrupt the natural order. Eventually, we suffer for this. When, however, we remember our creative partners and act in concert, blending our human wills with the will of nature, then we have the potential to create a heaven on Earth, not just for ourselves but for all life. This, in a nutshell, is the message of the devas, their invitation to us to reclaim our true creative heritage by recognising our common spiritual ties with the spirituality of the world around us. Through Dorothy's experiences and words, this nutshell becomes filled with a rich and nourishing meat of ideas and new perspectives.

In the realm of occult literature, there are other books on the devas, but I find Dorothy's unique. Often, these formative forces or invisible overlords of nature are presented as awesome entities, surrounded by glamour and majesty—the stuff of fairy tales. Sometimes, they are made to be simply cute. At other times, they are presented as beings or forces to be magically controlled and manipulated.

What Dorothy presents is a picture of another kingdom of life co-equal to our own, filled with wisdom and power, but not all-wise or all-powerful; in fact, they seek blending with humanity, recognising areas in which we are more skilled, more wise, more powerful than they. They are awesome, yet approachable. They are co-creators, not pawns to be summoned and used. They have never left 'the Father's house' nor lost the inner knowledge of God; a revitalised look at divinity is something they offer. But neither have they experienced the depths of involvement with matter, the dilemmas of free will, the bittersweet taste of individuality. We have much to offer them.

In short, it is partnership that this book speaks about, and mutual enhancement. Other cultures more ancient than ours knew of these beings and often dealt with them, the native American cultures being a good example. However, we have confronted the experience and challenges of power in our industrial culture as no other peoples have in history. Out of this can come an understanding of what it means to be a formative force, a planetary influence. Out of our experiences, transmuted and realigned with spirit, we can meet the devas as brothers, as partners, as co-creative equals and learn from each other. It is an exciting promise.

Dorothy is, as you will soon discover, a person who in herself blends these two worlds to make that promise real. Down-to-earth, practical, not given to glamour, nevertheless she has learned to expand her spirit and step beyond the purely human points of view without abandoning them either. Knowing her has been a great privilege in my life; offering her book to you is another. She offers the light of a reunion; may it always illumine our future.

*To learn to talk
with angels is really a way
of learning how to talk
with ourselves and with
each other in new and profoundly deeper ways.*

Chapter 1

Introduction

Yes, I talk with angels, great Beings whose lives infuse and create all of Nature. In another time and culture I might have been cloistered in a convent or a temple, or, less pleasantly, burnt at the stake as a witch. In our sceptical time and culture, such a claim is more likely to be met with scoffing disbelief or as the ramblings of a dreamy female. Being a practical, down-to-earth person, I had never set out to learn to talk with angels, nor had I ever imagined that such contact would be possible or useful. Yet, when this communication began to occur, it did so in a way that I could not dispute.

Concrete proof developed in the Findhorn garden, which became the basis for the development of the Findhorn Community. This garden was planted on sand in conditions that offered scant hospitality and encouragement for the growth of anything other than hardy Scottish bushes and grasses requiring little moisture or nourishment. However, through my telepathic contact with the angelic Beings who overlight and direct plant growth, specific instructions and spiritual assistance were given. The resulting garden, which came to include even tropical varieties of plants, was so astonishing in its growth and vitality that visiting soil experts and horticulturists were unable to find any explanation for it within known methods of organic husbandry, and eventually had to accept the unorthodox interpretation of angelic help.

To learn to talk with angels is really learning to talk with ourselves and with each other in new and profoundly deeper ways. It is learning how to communicate with our universe more openly and how to be more in tune with our role as co-creators and participate in its evolution. Modern communication has developed marvellously and very quickly in a physical, technological mode, but other deeper and more subtle forms of communication remain untapped. For the future of our world and ourselves, we must now begin to use those deeper forms. It is from my experience of doing this that I want to share my findings with others so that they too can enter into this communication, which is really a communion with the essence and joy and power of life.

To do this is not a matter of technique. I have no easy methods which can teach you to talk with angels or with your deeper self in ten lessons or in two weekends. People in industrial cultures seem to expect and desire instant gratification, but true communication arises out of our own being and from the wholeness of our lives. It is more something that we become over the course of our existence and less something that we learn. What we really communicate is what we are, not so much what we can say in words. To communicate with angels really requires a particular attitude of wholeness towards life, towards others and towards ourselves. I cannot teach this, but I can show through my own life and experiences what this attitude is and how it developed and expressed itself in me.

I maintain that any of us can talk with angels. The fact that I, with my very human hang-ups and perceptions, learned to do it, means that the path is available for anyone else who is willing to change orthodoxies and explore his or her world in new ways. It requires a joyful enlargement of our view of reality, a readiness to be open to ourselves and our environment, and a conscious movement to embrace our own wholeness.

*Though I speak
with the tongues of men
and angels, and have not
love, I am become
as sounding brass, or tinkling cymbal.*

I Corinthians 13, v.1

Chapter 2

Growing Up

My background was thoroughly stable and supportive, but beyond that it was normal enough. I had exceptionally fine, caring parents, who were loved and respected by all who knew them. We lived in a small Canadian city in an old house on top of a hill. Our home, in which my father had grown up, was set among trees, surrounded by lawns and rough land, with a flower and vegetable garden adjoining a wild wood.

My first vivid memory is of the birth of self-consciousness. Until then, I am told, I was a bright happy child, but a moment of embarrassment in kindergarten when I realised that I had been completely misunderstood led me to consider the world as not with me and therefore against me. In that moment I fell heavily out of Eden, and changed into an awkward, unhappy little person.

However, like all children I lived fairly fully in the present, when a year or a day seem equally long. The seasons came and went, gaining distinctive lustre in the extreme climate of Ontario. Each season was my favourite at the time: the white beauty of winter snow with its sporting games, the rushing abundance of spring, the heat and holidays of the summer, and the flaming colours and smoky smells of autumn. I loved to explore the woods adjoining our property, to ski there in the winter and discover the first wild flowers in the spring. Our home, with its ready-made playgrounds and the welcome of my parents, was a mecca for the neighbouring kids as well as for my two brothers and me. Unlike most of our friends, we had little money, but in the richness of the family nest we felt no sense of lack. I was quite happy to save to buy a bicycle. Besides, the public library offered the world of books, which captured me early, feeding an innate sense of adventure and turning me into an avid reader.

But did this benign environment make me happy? Far from it. Happiness depends upon the relationship of one's inner being to one's surroundings. At the age of eight I can remember feeling sure that I, or anyone else, could be and do whatever we wanted. But imperceptibly that inner strength became submerged in the self-conscious embarrassments that accompany adolescence. Early at-home dances were severe ordeals, with boys and girls lined up on opposite sides of the room, too shy even to smile (at least I was). I felt awkward, limited, and inadequate.

When I was seventeen the opportunity arose, thanks to a kind aunt, to choose a career and study at University. Though I had a hankering to be an artist, I decided against art because I knew I had talent but not genius. After weighing the pros and cons of several courses of study, I chose an eminently practical business course which offered a B.A. degree in a concentrated three rather than the usual four years. Moving to the University of Western Ontario brought a new start, an opportunity to widen my circle of friends, to break old patterns and deprecating self-images. Since there were no student residences, I joined a sorority, with girls I considered balanced, sporty executive types rather than those I regarded as either wealthy socialites or quiet grinds. Although the academic side of life offered no great difficulties, typing and shorthand were a constant trial. I was hopelessly poor in these subjects, being too tense and self-concerned to pass the practical tests, which didn't increase my fondness for them. Badminton became my non-academic outlet, and I made the four-girl team in my first year.

Like most students, we questioned and argued about who we were and about the goals and purpose of life. I had not found answers to these questions in the Sunday School teachings, sermons and services of the Presbyterian Church of Canada, which my family attended but did not force on me. The unobtrusive integrity of my parents supplied me with the best teaching of all, but did not satisfy me intellectually. For me the traditional religious concepts of God had little connection with the deeper questions of life. I believed truth was no respecter of creeds. But our discussions at University brought me no closer to understanding truth, and I remember sadly concluding that there were no answers, otherwise we would have read or heard of them. In those days neither bookshops nor libraries carried works on the esoteric or occult mysteries of life, or even on other world religions. However, I do have a vague memory of a book about an Eastern teacher which delighted me with the breadth of its philosophy.

The expectation of my family was that I would seek employment as a trained secretary after University, then eventually marry and settle down. I too took this for granted, but by the time I graduated and got a job the Second World War had broken out, and my generation was jolted out of the usual pattern. My yearnings for greener pastures awoke. When I discovered that the British Security Coordination was recruiting Canadian secretaries for work in New York, my staid job in a Toronto insurance office became even more tedious. New York! But that was in another country, and besides, I knew no one there. Though I listened cautiously as friends and relatives alike warned me of the loneliness and isolation of big, strange cities, I still wanted to go. Not until the one friend who had actually travelled, quietly said, 'Try it. It would be good for you,' did I decide to set out.

Because I was barely twenty-one, the employment agency arranged for me to travel with a chaperone from Union Station in Toronto. There I met Sheena, a Scottish woman seven years my senior who was to have a major influence on my life, but at the time I was aware only of her obvious *savoir faire* and delicate Gaelic beauty. Together, we took the train to New York. All I remember about that journey was my worry about how much to tip the porter!

New York was glamorous and exciting to my eyes: I loved the sophisticated Fifth Avenue shops, bargains at Gimbels' base-

9

ment, the new-found interest of live theatre, the skyscrapers and the many ethnic restaurants. My job with the British Intelligence Service was even more intriguing when I found that it was so confidential that I could tell nobody what I was doing. I walked the New York streets on that first day, pinching myself to make sure that I really was engaged in such fascinating work. (The book, A Man Called Intrepid, later made such work public.) Of course, I was only a secretary, but the material handled was a long way from the mundane practicalities of insurance letters, and our bosses were mainly Englishmen who seemed very accomplished and cultured to me.

After a few weeks, Sheena and I found our own companions. She found friends with musical and cultural interests, while I teamed up with Betty, a Toronto woman who also enjoyed badminton. Betty and I took every opportunity to explore New York together and, soon enough, even more of the world. Hearing of vacancies for secretaries in Panama, we volunteered and became the first of many to leave New York for government work in southern countries.

Panama was for us an exuberant array of exotic hothouse flowers, jungles, daily tropical cloudbursts, pink gins and frantic social life. The hundreds of U.S. Army personnel posted to the Canal Zone all seemed to want dates, and I experienced a new-found popularity. Betty and I tried to continue our globe-trotting when we were offered various other posts, first by a former boss of mine who had moved to Guatemala. Then we were lured by tales of Haitian voodooism, and of a wonderful home in a yacht among coral reefs off British Honduras. Head Office responded to our efforts with a cable which, when decoded, read 'This is not, repeat not, a travel agency.'

Working with us in the Panama office was a young man named John who was considered eccentric. An untidy redhead who kept to himself and delighted in secrecy, he had succeeded in clouding even his nationality with mystery, for no one knew whether he was English or Norwegian. Stories of him circulated about the office, such as that he had once been seen to sit for hours cross-legged on a beach for who-knows-what reason. This kind of thing intensified my interest in him. I remember talking with him one evening when he presented Atlantis to me, not as myth or fantasy, but simply and matter-of-factly as a chapter in history. Such conversations reawakened in me those unanswered questions of University days, and John's answers rang true.

I enjoyed his company, but when he eventually asked me to marry him, I refused because of my lack of knowledge of him, because I could see his faults, and because people were warning me against him, suspicious of his oddity. Moreover, I was still savouring the joys of popularity. Soon John began asking me *when*, not *if*, I would marry him. His arrival by my desk one day with a telegram posting him to Buenos Aires triggered in me, to my amazement, a new and mysterious experience. In a sudden flash of intense clarity I knew that I had to marry him. All my mental reservations temporarily vanished and, though they rose again almost immediately, my new perception powerfully overruled them. Besides, there was no time, for that moment led to a frantic week of arranging our wedding at the Cathedral in the Canal Zone, organising a reception and putting our passports in order. By the time I finally sat back, married, I was flying with him to the Argentine, having at least discovered that he was English.

John and I both loved travelling, and the volatile life of the Latin American countries provided us with many new encounters, even a live revolution. Because it was wartime, our main focus was British government work which involved us in long hours each day with little free time. Gradually, I became aware that there was an additional, and very important, aspect of John's life which he was not sharing with me. This was brought to a head one night when I awoke to find the bed empty beside me and John seated cross-legged in the living room shrouded in quietude. In the morning when I attempted to question him indirectly—I was afraid of silencing him forever by my directness—there was no acknowledgement, no response at all. I became increasingly disturbed by this secrecy but, in my helplessness, I could only accept it. As part of this process of acceptance, I found myself at one point sitting in a park in Rio de Janeiro, where John had left me while he went to visit some friends. I spent the afternoon wandering about, getting lost and trying to find my way back to our meeting place. Meanwhile John, as it turned out, was confronting the insistence of his friends that he bring me to meet them, which he eventually did.

Shabaz and Nuria were teachers in the Sufi Order, a spiritual discipline unknown to me. We attended their service of Universal Worship, a ceremony which included readings of similar passages from such holy books as the Bhagavad Gita, the Bible and the Koran. Here at last was an expression of my own belief in the universality of truth; and here at last was a clue to John's interests.

Shabaz showed me a photograph of an East Indian, saying, 'Of course, you know him.' 'No,' I replied, 'Who is he?' With a reproachful look at John, Shabaz declared, 'His name is Hazrat Inayat Khan. He is the greatest man since Jesus.' I made no reply, but I immediately rejected a statement so contrary to my cultural conditioning. Jesus Christ was the only Begotten Son of God, and while that statement had no meaning to me, it was evidently too deeply ingrained to be discarded. However, other aspects of what I was told were very satisfying to me, and I was grateful when Shabaz initiated me into this esoteric order. I was given mantras, breathing exercises and study papers. Later I read various lectures by Inayat Khan and found them deeply appealing in their wise simplicity. They spanned a breadth of subjects, and taught that in the midst of life man's purpose is to become God-conscious.

Why had John not shared something so essential not only to his life but to mine as well? He explained that he had not considered it right for a husband to influence his wife in spiritual matters. I couldn't really accept this explanation. Perhaps he was genuinely afraid of obscuring my motives. I didn't know then, and still don't. But I was happy that we could now share this aspect of life together, and grateful that through him my life had taken a new and significant turn. I see now that in accepting Sufism I chose to make spiritual unfoldment the focus of my life. Sufism, like other teachings I embraced along the way, pointed me inwards, always inwards.

Seeking more active participation in the war, John and I

left South America for London. There we explored many of the 'spiritual' groups in Britain. Most of these I found interesting but either rigid, exclusive or too sweet for my taste. We also contacted and worked with Sufis in the area and, because Hazrat Inayat Khan had been introduced to me as being in somewhat the same category as Jesus Christ (though to me an unacceptable comparison) I began to probe his life. Secretly and critically I searched for any inconsistency between his actions and his teachings, which I now valued. For four years I questioned people who had known him. It was not so much what they said that began to change my attitude, but the fact that the very mention of his name powerfully affected them. Even the most flinty matron softened and became loving when remembering him. I could find nothing derogatory, and finally I had to accept him as a truly Christ-illumined being. In my search I formed my own understanding of what that meant: that a Christ-illumined being is one who is conscious of the divinity in all things and thinks, feels and acts from that centre of wholeness. Inayat Khan's embodiment of that principle served to demonstrate that such a consciousness can be achieved even today, and his humanity brought God and man closer together for me.

Then Sheena came into my life again, and our relationship began to develop on a new level. Since my life had assumed a spiritual focus, I was now open to a similar side of her, a side I had been unaware of in New York. She had come from a Quaker background and, for her, New Testament teaching was a living reality. A natural mystic who even as a child sought union with God, her own inner experiences were difficult for her to interpret within the framework of traditional Christianity. Through John's knowledge she was helped to recognise her experiences within the pattern of occult traditions, which deepened her understanding of herself and of what she was beginning to see as her teaching. I Corinthians chapter 13 was her Bible: 'Though I speak with the tongues of men and of angels and have not love . . . ' Love was not just a beautiful concept to her; it was an imperative to action. To her the Divine was within all things and had to be expressed in our daily lives. 'Love does not seek to hold, but to give,' she would tell us, and her love went out

13

immediately to anyone or anything in need. With an intuitive knowing, she would often telephone someone at the critical moment when they required help.

One incident exemplified for me the breadth of her love. She and I went to a Fair and wandered into the flea circus where two fleas (so tiny that down feathers had been attached to them for the sake of visibility) were being forced to race each other. Sheena expressed tremendous concern and compassion for the way that these two seemingly insignificant creatures were being treated, and her consideration struck a deep chord in me. To her, every aspect of life was worthy of love.

With Sheena I began to come to terms with the practical implications of love in action. This signalled a new phase in my development. I was beginning to see that life had a plan, a purpose and a progression, that each person was evolving constantly towards a finer attunement with higher principles. But the experiences that I would have to go through in order to fuse these concepts into my being were fortunately beyond my surmise, and certainly were not what I would have chosen, for the whole course of my life was to be altered radically.

My marriage was not living up to my ideals. John, in spite of what I considered to be his superior mental and spiritual powers, was exceedingly selfish, and treated me so casually that new acquaintances were puzzled to hear that we were married. He expressed none of the sharing love which I thought that the close relationship of marriage would include. I reacted by becoming more and more mouse-like, repressing all my resentment at his treatment. After all, our partnership had in one sense not been my personal choice; an extraordinary inner knowledge had ordained it. John may have felt the same way about it, since he took our marriage for granted. However, I had now learned to love him and had become very dependent on him.

Sheena saw the situation very clearly and in her wish to help, sought guidance from her inner sources. She received a message for me, which in essence asked me if I were willing to give John up for his own sake, to help him realise the realities and responsibilities of human relationships, love and marriage. I trusted and loved Sheena, but not sufficiently to accept this shattering suggestion, which had actually never occurred to me and which brought up in me a tremendous fear of a life without him. In that message, however, was a reminder that I should act on my highest experience of love.

I remembered that this experience, which had made a deep impression on me but which had been so personal that I had shared it with no one, not even Sheena, had happened when John and I were making love. Instead of reaching an orgasm, I had suddenly been shot into another realm, another state of consciousness where everything was incredibly beautiful, where evil did not and could not exist, where I was so blissfully happy that I wished to remain forever. But below my ecstasy I could hear John calling me, and I had been presented with the choice of whether to stay, or whether to leave my new-found heaven because he needed me on Earth. I had chosen to return to him. Recalling this experience made me realise that I had, similarly, to leave what seemed to me a high state—my being with John— again, for his sake.

Why was it for his sake? I did not precisely know, but I had learned to trust Sheena's guidance and had already realised that John had a long pattern of simply running away when relationships became difficult for him. Having a wife gave him an excuse for not facing or finalising relationships with other women. Although divorce was not mentioned in the message, I also realised that I was being tested as to my willingness to be unselfish and to give up my most cherished possession, John, if he chose freedom from our marriage, as I knew possessiveness was not part of true love. I hoped divorce would not result, and Sheena later told me that she had no expectation of divorce. But I had to be willing; that was my test. Only if I could face what in my mind was the worst alternative (divorce) would I fully know whether I could act from a state of unpossessive love.

My problem was that I didn't think that I was capable of going through with a divorce, and of 'sacrificing' myself in this way, yet I knew that was what I had to be prepared to do. I was alone in London, while John was in blockaded Berlin where, he said, wives were not allowed. I was desperate: I had the motive and tremendous energy for achieving an unselfish,

15

undemanding and giving love, to be expressed by my willingness for a divorce if necessary, but *how* was I to achieve that unselfish willingness?

I turned to a series of Sufi teachings called 'Sadhana', or how to achieve a goal. I knew my goal, and I hoped that these study papers would help me to reach it. They did, by outlining various methods. One suggestion was to tell no one what one's goal is. Then, of course, no one could send you any thoughts and no one would apply pressure of any kind. I faithfully followed this suggestion and did not tell even my parents about my problems and my aims. Another suggestion in these papers was to hold the image of the goal in one's mind, never letting any doubt destroy it, otherwise one would have to start from scratch to rebuild it. I was torn in two—on the one hand believing myself capable of divorcing John, and on the other hand assailed by doubts as my sense of lack, my fear of failing or my desire to be with him arose strongly. I prayed for strength to follow my assignment, and I saturated myself with these teachings, spending my evenings for months concentrating on reading, re-reading and again reading these helpful hints to achieve success. I channelled all my energy toward my positive goal, strengthening the higher side of my nature and turning my back as much as I could on the pull of my fears.

Top right:
Like all children I lived fairly fully in the present . . .

Bottom right:
The unobtrusive integrity of my parents supplied me with the best teaching of all.

16

*. . . he eventually asked me to
marry him.*

*. . . I met Sheena . . . who was to
have a major influence in my life*

18

*With a clarity
that extended beyond time into eternity,
I knew that God was within.
God was no distant figurehead
defined by ideals and philosophies;
God was within me, the core of my life,
real, ever-present,
inseparable.*

Chapter 3

Growing In

During this gruelling period I felt very much on my own, and I was acutely aware of a deeply ingrained sense of inadequacy. I know now that we are constantly changing, moving and growing, but most of the time I think that we don't notice such changes. We women in particular often walk with uncertain steps as if on quicksand, erratically depending for direction on feelings, mundane particulars or the wisdom of others. However well-intentioned we may be, the blurred edges of thought and action betray us. A sneaking suspicion that we are really just fumbling and inchoate, that we lack peace and poise, is endlessly affirmed. However hard we may try to chisel away at ourselves through study, introspection or encounter groups, through prayer or meditation, we remain our limited selves. But now and then, somehow, through a grace beyond comprehension, we break out of this self-perpetuating cycle, touch another dimension of understanding and become filled with a new realisation. From that moment of birth we are in a new framework; we can never return to our old views of ourselves and life. Although habitual moulds may tend to obscure that moment of clarity, from then on our problems and challenges assume a different aspect. At least, this is my experience of the human 'split'. Such a moment of revelation happened to me one evening in my London apart-

21

ment.

I was sitting at the kitchen table drinking the milky coffee I had learned to enjoy in England. Separated from my husband and living alone for the first time, I was very conscious of the problems of the life I had chosen. I was a creature of massive dilemmas, striving to become more loving and whole than I believed was possible for myself, when suddenly, out of the blue, with a clarity that extended beyond time into eternity, I knew that God was within. God was no distant figurehead defined by ideals and philosophies; God was within me, the core of my life, real, ever-present, inseparable. In a moment I was myself again, but more than myself, forever more than myself. I had experienced reality for the first time.

I cannot remember whether I got up and danced, or wept with joy, or sat there numb with wonder. I do remember that when a friend at the art school which I was attending saw me the next day, she exclaimed, 'You are different. Something has happened to you. Why, even your voice has changed!' I could only smile at her with happy eyes. I couldn't explain, I still can't explain what God is, though I have used many words since then to describe similar experiences. But at that time I just knew it, and I walked on air for weeks in the memory of that divine reality.

That unsolicited moment of glory has since given birth to other such moments. It has been described elsewhere as the First Initiation or, in Christian terms, the birth of the Christ child in the heart. I am not suggesting that it is a particularly unique occurrence. I believe that many people experience it—in different ways, of course—and that these experiences are the basis upon which a new world—a new age—is arising. It became the core of my actions, when I let it, for my personality often pulled me in apparently opposite directions. In my everyday life I experienced a division in myself, which was accentuated by the constantly reiterated social mores of my time, yet, in that instant in my London apartment I experienced a vast unity.

While touching that centre gave me a great high, paradoxically it seemed to amplify the difference between the two realities. Yet in a strange way that inner presence excluded nothing but enfolded all extremes. Our lives encompass highs and lows, inners and outers, positives and negatives. We perceive duality and are tossed about by the pairs of opposites, with only a certain freedom to choose, until we blend sufficiently with the 'higher' to see that the 'lower' is a vital part of the process, and that these apparently conflicting forces interact to generate the dynamic that lifts us into the vast unity which we are. Then we can understand the meaning of 'resist not evil'; we can accept that whatever comes to us is necessary for our own development; and we can reconcile our two halves. Then we can also recognise that our 'higher' self is indeed angelic, and may even find, as I did, that we are walking with the angels.

My experience naturally made all the difference in my immediate life. I was soon ready to take action with John. I poured my soul into a letter to him, saying that without love in action our marriage was a sham, and that I was leaving for Canada to set him free to choose whether to build a new marriage with me or to separate from me. I hoped my actions would bring him to his senses. I had planned to leave this letter in our apartment for him on his return from Berlin, by which time I would be on the seas on my way to New York. But John, always intuitive, arrived in London with two airplane tickets to Canada in his hand on the day before I was due to sail. His arrival completely upset me and my plans. I had no idea whether to fly with him or take the boat. Perhaps the two tickets for a joint holiday indicated that he had had a change of heart, but perhaps not. I had to know, definitely. All those months of effort could not be wasted now by a wrong choice. I was in an agony of indecision. My back was truly against the wall and no one could help me.

At the first moment alone, instinctively and desperately, I implored an answer from within. In immediate, flawless clarity I received the name of the ship, 'Media'. The intensity of my desire to know had broken through something, and thereafter I knew that we could always find answers from within when we truly sought them. Immediately, all my burdens dropped away. On the following day the hundred and one things that I had to accomplish before departing were effortlessly and joyfully com-

23

pleted, as they always are when we are in harmony with our higher natures. The week's trip by boat was a wonderful holiday, and there to meet me on the wharf was a penitent John. However, I could not accept that our marriage was a going concern until he proved it. He soon returned to Berlin while I, after visiting my parents, went to stay with a Sufi friend.

Erica and her two small sons were living in Southern California near a group called 'The School of the Natural Order', led by an American teacher called Vitvan. We would start each day by walking over a mountain and through orange groves to hear Vitvan speak at six a.m. It was a pleasant walk, if sometimes a very dark one at that hour, and our differing natures are perhaps well exemplified in the following characteristic exchange. Erica, who was exuberantly joyful at all times, would make remarks like, 'Oh, look, the moon is out!' I, still half asleep, would grumpily reply, 'Any fool can see the moon is out.' Nonetheless, we spent a fruitful year imbibing Vitvan's teachings, which were a combination of Shakti Yoga and such Western concepts as Einstein's theories and Korzybski's science of semantics. We particularly appreciated various maxims of Vitvan: 'Don't react, act,' or 'Don't alibi' (i.e. don't find some excuse for your own misdemeanours). However, he had a peculiar penetrating laugh that made us wince, and for this irrational reason neither of us ever fully accepted him as our teacher. Nevertheless, we did pick up a stock of pseudo-scientific/ psychological/semantic jargon with which we self-righteously blasted and flattened our long-suffering friends when we returned to England in June 1950. Now, thirty years later, I have come across Vitvan's teachings again, and can understand and appreciate them more fully.

By letter, or lack of letters, John had shown no signs of new love and caring. He had said he wanted a truly loving relationship with me, but as he was not practising it I knew I had to take action. Therefore, unknown to him, I went to Berlin to find legal grounds for divorce. In an incredible month, in which I seemed to be upheld in a stream of energy in the most extraordinary way, we thoroughly explored our situation. Although John was in love with someone in the Berlin office, he said at first he didn't want a divorce, for such feeble reasons as, for example, that he didn't want to hurt my parents, for whom he had an exceptional regard, or, what would people think? Finally we achieved a clear ending of our relationship, agreed to separate and arranged the necessary legal grounds. We finished with a tour of Europe, which we both considered a honeymoon experience at the end instead of at the beginning of our union. Freed from ties to each other, we could fully enjoy one another. I felt a great sense of achievement, mixed with pangs of anguish whenever I saw a couple together, for I still did not consider the single state blessed.

The final divorce papers took a year, during which time I returned to art school for another term. Although unaware of it at the time, looking back I can see that my life had indeed changed. Through John, I had encountered Sufism and had been given a conscious spiritual focus in my life. This new focus had been strengthened by my contact with Vitvan and Sheena, while my inner experience of Divinity had brought a new dimension of reality to my beliefs. I had begun to act from inner directives, as I had done in both my marriage and my divorce, whereas previously I had tended to operate on the rational level, carefully analysing the pros and cons before embarking on any course of action. I now found myself experiencing a new freedom but, at the same time, confronting some basic questions.

On the mundane level, I had sufficient funds at that time to maintain myself without working. On another level, I had achieved my goal of loving John unselfishly, which had taken much of my energy for a time, and so I was free to direct that energy elsewhere. But where precisely was it to go? What was my role in life? What was I, Dorothy, to do, and what was my place in the divine plan? I decided to concentrate on answering these questions. For several months, while I kept myself physically occupied by completely redecorating my London apartment, I pondered. No insights emerged. Finally I realised that I must give in order to get, that by doing something I would learn what was best to do. I decided to get a job, but not a secretarial one.

I considered joining a church-associated organisation termed 'Moral Welfare'. My concept of morals was derived from Inayat Khan, i.e. conducting oneself for the highest good. Their concept, I soon realised, was helping women with illegitimate babies to uplift their sexual standards. Ironically enough, as a divorcee my previous marital experience was considered beneficial, but if I were to remarry this would have rendered me unfit. These moral niceties were too complex for me, and I settled for a philanthropic organisation, where I became involved in sending agricultural directives to a village in India. But soon I wondered what right I had, while sitting in London, to tell people in India what was best for them. This experience clarified my belief that change comes from within, that we can best help society by interacting with it. Thus ended my 'do-good' period. I returned to the business world as a secretary.

My connections with Sheena were now becoming closer, and much of my spare time was spent with her and others drawn to her, including Eileen and Peter Caddy. Peter was a good-looking Royal Air Force officer who had been devoted to Sheena for some years, having chosen to follow her teaching of love rather than his own British Rosicrucian training in the power of positive thought. Eileen, unlike me and my previous friends, was a domesticated, motherly person without intellectual pursuits, and neither she nor Peter were people towards whom I would have naturally gravitated. Eileen and I, and another friend of Sheena's called Gillian, were thrown together all the more when Peter was posted to the Far East. Many evenings after work I would go to Sheena's apartment, where she would give talks which I would take down in shorthand. These talks would be expansions of Christian teaching on love. I remember one on the puzzling concept of Christhood, on Christ being an office, not a person, but open to all who developed to a certain state. We were beginning to see Sheena more as a teacher than a friend. Without discouraging this development, she emphasised that the true teacher was within each one of us, and that the time would come when outer teachers would not be necessary.

Sheena's teachings always related directly to our lives.

Once, when I was dusting her furniture and thinking that chore boring and time-wasting, she gave me feedback on how upsetting my thoughts were, and asked me to leave. I was annoyed at having been so accurately caught out in my thoughts, but after that, whenever I found myself doing something without love, I remembered that incident and tried to change, aware that my surroundings were affected by my frame of mind. Generally, her own example was the most effective teaching. At that time she considered life to be a joyous adventure, and would express this. In fact my fondest memory of her was seeing her doing an impromptu dance in her small apartment as joy overflowed from her and she gaily leapt about like an enchanting elf.

In return for the help and teaching Sheena gave us, we rendered her what service we could. Once, when she was ill, we found that healing came through our hands, in a different way for each of us, and we would invoke healing for her.

At that time, when alone in my apartment, a recurring thought kept coming: stop, listen; stop, listen, write. I ignored that thought until it became so insistent that I was forced to listen (if only tentatively, because my critical mind allowed me to write only trite safe truths). I kept these sketchy writings to myself, until Sheena found out about them. After reading them carefully, she told me that they were truly inspired and asked why I didn't put their suggestions into action. With her encouragement, some inner floodgates opened to the most delightful, joyous thoughts and feelings. To me their source was God, because the inspiration derived from the same sort of place, or non-place, as that first experience of the God within; but in their joyousness, they were unlike anything I had ever encountered as being attributed to God. My initial inner experience had come unsought, but now I could return consciously to that wonderful, inner Presence, which was always different yet always the same.

Looking back, I would say that my mind was disposed to this process, in that Sheena received messages in a similar fashion and Eileen was beginning to write down daily guidance. Through Sufi exercises, I had learned a certain amount about concentration, which helped me to focus. After spells of mind wandering

I had to keep refocusing, and sift thoughts and feelings clearly before putting them into words. I heard no actual voice; there was a delicate and pure inner prompting which I tried to convey in my own words, as my art form. I wrote the words in short-hand while experiencing them, never losing awareness of my external environment. Although the writings later broadened into a more familiar mystical stream, I was particularly fond of the light early ones, like the rather frivolous:

> *Leading a life of bliss entails cancelling other engagements you have made through habit to your body, to convention and the social code, and to others' opinions. Throw these away merrily and fill your engagement book with my engagements, which may not be conventional but which are much more fulfilling. Each day is a blank page, and each hour should have a star to mark it as 'well spent'—stars of different colours but all of the same size, for if the hour is spent as I have planned, is one moment more important than another?*

Of course I doubted these writings. My mind said that it was nonsense that God would talk, for example, about 'quick-silver thoughts passing from his lips.' But Sheena was delighted, and gave me a schedule of sitting three times a day for the purpose of attuning to this inner Presence—always beginning by asking for cleansing and purifying. Without that schedule I would not have bothered with times of quiet, especially in my Fleet Street office. I would have continued with my usual activities, for the personal side of me resisted and did not want to listen. 'Why me?', I would ask. 'Why can't I have an ordinary life?' Perhaps the high joy and love of those times too painfully underlined the meagreness of my usual concepts of self. Yet in the presence of my resplendent God-self I was transformed: softened, awed, enlarged, beautified. Most times I sought no specific advice, but tuned in without knowing what would come. Naturally I would ask and get answers to personal problems, but generally I received different variations on the theme of love. Sometimes familiar ideas were presented, sometimes new ideas that seemed familiar. Of course, everything had to be filtered through the network of my own understanding. Sometimes the inner 'voice' said things that I hadn't heard before, like:

This morning the sun shines on the pages on which you are writing and casts long, flickering shadows. Most of what man does casts long shadows and, as in Plato's myth, he believes these shadows to be reality and he daily infuses fresh life into them. When he refuses to believe any longer in them, the pattern of light and dark will become less and less distinct, and gradually will blur into lightness. You will still have a world of contrasts, but the contrasts will be of colour, not black and white, and in change, not the darkness cast through heaviness. The range of the light will be immensely greater, and the surfaces will not only reflect but will give out light from within. The surfaces themselves are not static; this will be a moving picture and impossible for the artist to paint with his present materials. The artists will be artists in living, and the canvas will be as broad as the universe. . . .

Some messages referred to the receiving process. I was told, for example, that *'These words are impressed on your mind with such delicacy that the slender thread connecting them with my mind becomes soluble to any disturbance. Therefor choose a quiet time, and you must choose to make it silent.'*
I was often taken on a journey, as if I were travelling in space, as in:

The power of peace! The power of peace! What could be stronger than the peace that stays rooted and untouched by the tormented activity whirling about it?
Further in the depths of it you are unaware of the storms and are conscious of my peace as a gentle rain falling around you. Still further in and not a leaf rustles; it is as if the world were turned to stone and waiting, expectant, for even greater stillness. But further in still

the stoniness of the world has vanished, and there is movement again, the lightest and airiest and subtlest of blends, the faintest of sounds, only tinges of flashing colour—all contained in that unbreakable stillness.

Then that movement ceases and we pass to a formless world where lie waiting the seeds, the potencies, of all other worlds. This land you cannot sense, you cannot see nor hear, but you know that in its controlled vibrancy is the mighty bursting force of love eager for expression, waiting in the hollow of my hand in unprecedented peace. It is a tremulous world, where an entrance means surrendering to nothing, to everything, slipping in brim full of love and giving it up to the gossamer texture of you know not what, and in that surrendering being translated into a power stirring out of the depths of the God of love. . . .

The subjects discussed were always a surprise to me. In addition to the love themes, I had little essays on colour, on roses, on damask, on patience, on sex:

Think of what I accomplish through sex: the bringing to Earth of a soul. Life on Earth is very important to your growth. It is my testing ground, my escalator back to me, and the act that makes possible this sacred privilege is of boundless beauty to me. Nothing would exist without an act of creation, and perhaps that is why the limiting mind has degraded this act more than any other. In spite of this, somehow beauty is still touched, and it is painful to see that mountain of prejudice clamp down on a realisation of beauty and teach young ones to partake of the same unreality. This act should be regarded as a pinnacle of worship of me, and instead it is regarded as the bottom of all filth. . . .

I received some pretty sharp ideas to help me see the power of the mind, for I was very mentally oriented and needed pulling out of my rational ruts:

*The mind that tears to pieces, analyses, criticises, theorises,
is like cancer; the growth and life force are out of control.
... But because the world mind is distorted does not
mean that minds are of no avail. With my life force as their
source, you get a mind that regulates the universe and the
stars in their courses, down to the minute structure of a
grain of sand, so perfectly, so beautifully that every hair on
every head is numbered, destined, planned and coloured.*

At times the love experience was one of intimate, almost
devastating tenderness:

*Come closer, come closer, so softly, on tiptoe. As quietly
as a mouse creep up to me. Let me draw you nearer, in
slow motion lest we disturb anyone, lest we raise any dust.
Move closer to me, invisibly, hearing no evil, seeing no evil,
speaking no evil. Only purity can come close to me, and
we do not want any ripple of impurity to trip you.*
    *Draw nearer, draw nearer, with the movement of your
heart. Let it expand into me, let it bridge any space
between us, until there is just one big flowing heart, so
big that it holds up the universe. . . . Be part of my heart,
blood of my blood, my child. . . .*

Although most of the messages contained the phrase 'my
child', that phrase only echoed the pattern of my immediate
circle. God was a Father, in the vastness and omniscience of the
Presence, but He/She/It was much more, much closer, more a
Beloved, and became increasingly so. To counteract *my* tendency
to take refuge in outward action and others' opinions, there was
a constant emphasis on choosing the inner voice:

*The voice within is soft and loving, of an unbelievable
gentleness; the voices without are harsh, strident. The
voice within is full of love for you and everything; the
voices without are full of concern for the false self, false
values, for the things that lower the divinity in man. The
voice within speaks with singleness of purpose; the voices*

31

*without know not what they seek—first one thing, then
another, though all impair the dignity of man. The voice
within woos the soul to perfection; the voices without lead
blindly to destruction. The voice within speaks of beauty;
the voices without shriek coldly of facts. The voice within
holds truth as a kernel to cherish; the voices without twist
truth to a mould that will inflate all falseness. The voice
within concerns itself with the destiny of all; the voices
without are wholly concerned with the advancement of
one person. . . .*

This emphasis on heeding the inner voice made clearer
the reality of the inner universal world as a source for creative
action and eventually broadened my view to include the outer
world as an essential part of the process of our learning to be
whole.

The voice within led me to experience the essence of
things, e.g. the colour of blue, what is its essence? Is it the colour
of the coming dusk, the colour of peace? The voice within took
me on journeys into qualities other than that of peace, and at
the heart of them all was God, for God is the essence of everything. I met the essence of myself, of my uniqueness, and also
a vastness so infinite that I could not say it was myself. These
times of inner perception deepened and widened me, enriching
my life immeasurably. As God said, *'My beloved child, I am
leading you ever more deeply into love. I am doing it my way,
the perfect way, as I do with each soul.'*

Looking at those messages now, I see their limitations,
and also that they made me very aware of myself as a duality,
divided into higher and lower. But that too is part of the
process. We continually reach points where we have to choose
what part of ourselves to identify with, to choose to face the
sun and let our shadows fall behind. In choosing my inner
promptings, I had to put the fragmented part of myself behind
and look towards my whole self, the divine spark. I had done
that in choosing to embody an unpossessive love and bringing
that choice through in my divorce action, but to *maintain*
that nearness to my inner core seemed almost impossible. When

close to it, I was at ease with everything, then imperceptibly I would fall away. When I realised that I hadn't thought of God for ten hours, say, I would kick myself and feel guilty. But however far or long I fell, always that inner Presence, once contacted, filled the gap and completely satisfied me, and I would emerge, refreshed, renewed and guiltless. The reiterated *'Seek me first and all else will be added'* enhanced a tendency to live without plans.

These writings meant a great deal to Sheena too; she treasured them as she did those of Eileen, whose inner contact produced similar yet different messages. Eileen heard a definite voice in almost Biblical language. Sheena once called Eileen's messages 'bread and butter' and mine the 'dessert', and remarked that I was adding an element often absent from establishment Christianity, namely joy.

Altogether, it was a wonderful period of growth, although I was continually aware of the gulf between the high conscious-ness of spirit and my personality's deep sense of dullness, awkwardness and limitation. Yet the die was cast, and when Sheena suggested that I give up my lucrative, soft job on Fleet Street to live according to God's will, I was willing to make the attempt.

But what was God's will? How could I live it? We sought to be consciously attuned to the God within at all times, and to lead our lives according to its directives. In the chaotic period that followed I was to discover that many so-called unspiritual people were far more attuned than I was. Sheena suggested that I go into service. When I realised that this meant being a servant, I was shocked but amenable.

I took a job as second kitchen maid in an old people's home on the Hampshire coast. Here I learned much, and my pride took some interesting tumbles, for instance, when having to accept tips. One of my assignments was to lay breakfast trays for the old people, and the first kitchen maid, an almost illiterate Irish woman, trained me. She laid trays by instinct and could not instruct me in words, and I made numerous mistakes in my trial and error methods. I became very aware that she regarded me as extremely stupid. So much for my college degree!

33

There was a green baize door at this home through which a servant could not step unless at the bidding of the management. To step through this door, often to help someone, was an unheard-of encroachment, although the class barrier was maintained, it seemed to me, even more strongly by the servants than the masters. I literally stepped through this strict barrier to attempt to heal a patient and to paint one of the rooms in the rambling old house, eventually leaving with good feelings all around.

I then failed miserably as mother's help in the home of a Church of Scotland minister in Kirkcaldy (to whom I had arrogantly expected to bring a deeper understanding of Christianity) and fled back to the fleshpots of temporary secretarial work in London to recoup my finances. I had a sojourn as the matron of a girls' school near Chichester, for which I was singularly unfitted due to my complete ignorance of girls' schools. I did not know that Lysol should be diluted before it is applied to a cut, or that a girl with suspected mumps is best isolated from her class. In spite of this, I was invited back to work another term, but as secretary, not as matron. Perhaps they had enjoyed the comic relief of my efforts in the sick bay!

During these escapades my life was intertwining with Sheena's, with Peter and Eileen's, and with other of Sheena's followers. Sheena was having her problems and pressures, which became intolerable as she imposed upon herself the impossible mission of changing the world, a role that no one could fulfil; all we have the right to change is ourselves and *our* world. Her inability to bring about such a change eventually made her bitter and forceful, I think. But to me she will always be that dancing elf through whose encouragement I was able to touch the greatest treasure of all, the God within, whom she sought to serve with such intensity. The foundations for the next portion of my life, and those of Peter and Eileen's, were laid by her, by her love of God, her love of humanity, her vision, her sense of perfection, her dedication, and by the various lessons which brought out these points in our apprenticeship with her, and finally, by our having the strength to break with her and put our inner divinity first.

34

But before this was to happen, we experienced a really weird period. It began when one of Sheena's disciples left his wife, child, mother-in-law and job to be with Sheena. The mother-in-law was furious; she contacted the press with a garbled story of how her son-in-law had been purloined by a female religious teacher. In a bleak and newsless January in Scotland, the story caught on. Since we had no name and belonged to no organisation, some bright lad coined the phrase 'The Nameless Ones'. Reporters harried us all over Scotland, their stories growing to such proportions and being quoted so out of context that, for one crazy month, the activities of 'The Nameless Ones', fact and fiction, were headline news in most Scottish newspapers. We were really hounded. I remember being wakened at three a.m. by newsmen tapping on the windows, and on another day finding twenty reporters waiting for an interview at breakfast time, all with different newspapers to show me.

At first we talked freely, thinking that perhaps the publicity was to reveal a new way of life to a waiting public; but when we found that the facts were being distorted for their sensational value and that a woman 'Jesus Christ' was being derisively announced, we ceased talking. It was tough. Already we had lost or sold our possessions and had no money; now we lost our jobs, our reputations, and any friends we had left. Even our ideals seemed to have become confused. We became a hunted laughing-stock. This certainly confirmed my feelings that I had never *chosen* the spiritual life but had been kicked into it. I was fed up with the whole affair. When one of the reporters said, 'You shouldn't be with this lot' and offered me five pounds for a train trip to London away from it all, I accepted with alacrity. I had had enough of this freakish life and hated the publicity. Ultimately, I decided to leave Britain for a new start back in Canada.

First, I thought I should at least have the decency to tell Sheena of my decision. I headed for the Scottish Isles to find her. It was Christmas day, the day that most people spend happily and cosily with family and friends, and there was I, on the roads in frost and ice and wind, with all my worldly belongings in two suitcases, feeling utterly hopeless. I tried, and failed, to hitch a ride to Oban. Eventually a truck driver picked me up, adding the noise and clutter and draughts of his huge vehicle to my general misery. I missed the ferry; I missed everything. I reached the Isle of Mull in a state of depression to find Peter and Eileen about to leave for Glasgow. Sheena arrived and managed to persuade me to rethink my decison while staying in a little two-room cottage she had rented on an isolated bluff on Mull, overlooking the Isle of Iona.

Outside the cottage was a water pump; inside was a camp bed and a box. The toilet facilities were rocks and heather, the fireplace with its hanging kettle acted as both kitchen stove and heating, when fuel was available, and the dishes were six exquisite Rockingham plates. Winter gales and rain lashed about, but I enjoyed them. I like weather of all sorts, I love winds, the scenery was wildly beautiful, and being alone held no terror for me. Money was almost non-existent, but I was befriended by a simple, kindly neighbour. He became the main supplier of my food and fuel (peat), which he surreptitiously took from his parents. I occupied myself with my usual task of painting walls.

As had been the case after my divorce, I was at a point of freedom; but this time the experience was negative. Everything which had given meaning and purpose to my life had fallen away. My spiritual training seemed useless. I felt stripped even of God. Why had I gone through all this? Why were we still being hunted by reporters? After several months, during which I gained some little peace of mind, I knew that I could not run away, that my next step was to join Peter, Eileen and their two boys in Glasgow. With at least some understanding of how people can arrive at such a point of despair that nothing matters whatsoever, I arrived in Glasgow. Peter and Eileen were in a similarly subdued condition. I found temporary secretarial work. Peter sold brushes, and we lived very sparsely, our weekly treat being fish and chips on Saturday night. When Peter finally applied for and obtained the position of manager of a large hotel in the north of Scotland, I knew from within that I was to go there too.

The next six years were a settled period of both consolidation and preparation. At Cluny Hill Hotel, a great Victorian mansion open only in the summer, I worked as Secretary/Receptionist. It was interesting to see behind the scenes of a hotel, and to experience a group which both worked and lived under one roof. Although, in the shadow of our recent publicity, we kept silent about spiritual principles, inner guidance supplied the basis for the running of the hotel. An example comes to mind. Two hundred guests were expected shortly for dinner, and the head chef was drunk and useless — alcohol was a popular escape from stress for many of the staff. What were we to do? Guidance was sought and Eileen received the instructions: 'Peter is to give him another drink.' Peter did, whereupon the chef pulled himself together and coped magnificently with the situation. The guidance, although often unorthodox, always worked.

Gradually the hotel changed from its white elephant status into a popular, money-making concern. It also gave us opportunities to deal with people, to look after their creature comforts, including food and entertainment, and to create a group feeling among the staff. I undertook the redecoration of the quarters, which were in a disgraceful condition; the unruly hotel staff, contrary to the predictions of gossip mongers, responded to this care by keeping the rooms clean. The peaceful winter months we spent outside clearing the long-neglected grounds.

We continued our spiritual attunement and developed telepathic links in several areas, including what we called the Network of Light, which were centres throughout the world aligning to spirit. We also contacted space beings, even went as far as attempting a physical contact at a selected landing spot by raising our vibrations while they lowered theirs. We did this because we believed that rescue operations might be necessary in case man blew up our Earth with nuclear power. When we were told by our space friends that the danger was over, we immediately stopped such activity. Unknown to us, contact with beings from other planets and solar systems was occurring throughout the world at this time.

Sheena's teaching that at some point we would dispense with teachers came true when, knowing from within that our work was at the hotel at that time and having been told by the management that we would lose our jobs if we re-connected with Sheena, we refused her requests to let her stay with us or to follow her elsewhere. This cut the relationship and we saw little of her for the next few years. She died some time later, still misunderstanding, unfortunately, our seeming denial of her.

Later, we moved to the Trossachs Hotel and unsuccessfully attempted to build it up in the same manner as Cluny Hill Hotel. Our lack of success may have been the reason why the general manager of the hotel chain suddenly and for no given reason gave us four hours' notice to leave. (Personally, I believe she was weary of competing with God in the running of the hotels, and constantly being proven wrong.) We packed hurriedly, picked up the three boys at their school, and sought the only available roof, that of the Caddy caravan situated near the village of Findhorn.

To those who have
an insight into life,
everything has meaning.
To those whose eyes are open,
everything fits into place.

Chapter 4

Findhorn and
Angelic
Contact

The place to which our destiny had drawn us was certainly not our chosen place. The trailer park on Findhorn Bay was exceedingly ugly, especially after the luxurious space of the hotel. The park obviously had not developed as a tourist attraction, but as a functional base: the old World War runways, no longer used by the neighbouring RAF station of Kinloss, were perfect for rows of trailers. The inhabitants were mainly RAF personnel awaiting permanent accommodation or a posting overseas. Our own trailer at least had the advantage of being situated in a corner of the park in a hollow of gravel, gorse and broom.

Our immediate outlook was across many miles of flat land to distant hills, or to the sea. Once you saw beyond the initial bleakness, great beauty was revealed. The sky was always with us and we could not but be aware of it, for the constant wind brought a continuous cloud display, quiet or scudding, but always clouds in some shape, and the most magnificent sunsets I had ever seen. There was an odd gap in these clouds called the Kinloss Gap, so obvious and so remarkable that the RAF had built a Bomber Command base here during World War II to take advantage of the unusual blue skies which often made Kinloss the one clear landing spot in an otherwise overcast Britain. Time and again we would notice this phenomenon and enjoy the sunshine it brought.

Down the road along the Bay about a mile toward the sea lay Findhorn village. It is the third village with this name, the other two having been lost in time and the shifting sands of the area. It had grown up as a fishing village and had been a prosperous port for the Royal Borough of Forres in the days when there was a thriving trade between the north of Scotland and the northeast of Europe; and it had been linked by rail to Forres, five miles away, a link long since closed down. The houses are squat and huddled together, with tiny windows, no doubt as protection against the prevailing winds. Winds certainly prevailed; they are one of the outstanding characteristics of Findhorn. The rainfall is not great, only about 26 inches a year, yet I have seen those small cottages with permanent moisture soaking the inside walls. What to us was a decrepit, if picturesque, village was rapidly becoming a tourist centre as the old fishing folk — those whom the RAF had not provided with jobs — died and their houses were converted into summer residences for the wealthy of Inverness and Aberdeen.

Findhorn Bay is tidal and therefore ever changing, offering many magic moments. One such is to walk straight into the setting sun over the wet sands, which reflect all the rich colours of the glorious autumnal sunsets, on and on until one feels molten oneself. Another incomparable display comes when the rare winter frosts and tides mould the water, ceaselessly hardening it, carrying it, mixing it with sand, leaving abandoned thin ice sheets in all the tiny inlets or on rocks, rescuing them only to convert them into still more frosty shapes, all with the unerring natural patterns that must permeate the ethers. Every step on the Bay reveals to the eye a new white wonder: a combination of art unseen before; another aspect of the beauty of form; a transparency revealing still more intricate patterns underneath.

The Moray Firth was a mile away from us, over a stretch of gorse and heather moors and desolate sand dunes resembling a lunar landscape; the beach itself was deserted, continuing on from Findhorn village to the small town of Burghead nine miles away. Such is the individuality and character of these ancient places — Burghead has Roman ruins, proving that the Romans indeed did reach that part of the world by sea, not overland — that this insignificant settlement has a festival unique unto itself. The old New Year is celebrated in the latter part of January, by burning the clavie, an effigy which is paraded through the streets. I was continually amazed at the evidence of the past throughout Britain, no doubt because the indigenous people in my native Canada blended so well with the environment that there is little traceable past beyond that of our recent European or early American forebearers.

The Findhorn River, which empties into the Bay, has stretches of great beauty, combining granite rocks, peat-coloured torrents and majestic beech trees. It is a salmon river, netted at its mouth and in the bay in addition to being fished privately along its banks. Like other British rivers, the Findhorn is owned by various lairds, which is a good system insofar as the owners take responsibility for keeping their section of the river as pure and as well stocked with fish as possible. There are various crumbling castles in the area. Cawdor Castle, complete with legends, drawbridge and moat, was intact nearby, for we were in Macbeth country and several areas were the disputed sites of the Witches' Heath. In Forres itself was the Witch's Stone, covering the remains of the last witch rolled down in a barrel from Cluny Hill and buried in the spot, no doubt with a stake through her heart. Then too, there was the Sueno Stone, a large carved standing stone whose weathered runes were of great interest to archeologists and whose history is unknown. In the midst of this extravagant past were small towns inhabited by very practical and courteous Scots.

I had not expected to find rich agricultural land in that part of the world. I had romantic notions that the North of Scotland consisted of wild clan land and highlands, when in fact the Laigh of Moray has long been a famous granary and still has a high percentage grain yield per acre. A cluster of ancient ecclesiastical establishments is a reasonable indication of ancient wealth, and the Laigh is well dotted with old cathedrals, abbeys, priories, monasteries and nunneries. In fact, it has long been an area of spiritual and material abundance, and still has large areas of land with beautiful gardens owned by local lairds. Yet when we arrived, we discovered that across the bay, the last remaining portions of Britain's only desert were finally being conquered and planted by a system involving the cross-hatching of branches to protect seedling trees. That desert itself had been wealthy agricultural land until some few hundred years ago. Legend has it that, overnight, due to gales brought about as a punishment to a laird who had sold his soul to the devil, hundreds of acres of rich farm land and many dwellings were silted over. Today the Culbin Desert has become the Culbin Forest.

The reality of our own situation was more like a desert. The five Caddys filled the two tiny rooms of the trailer and I, thanks to the kindness of a hotel owner in the village, was allowed to sleep a mile or so away in the hotel staff quarters, which were closed for the winter. Each day I hiked across the dunes to spend the day with the Caddys. An extremely severe winter, well below freezing for six consecutive weeks — which incidentally froze every trailer water pipe in the park — made it necessary for me to go back to my room in the late afternoon just to turn on my electric underblanket. Otherwise it would have taken me hours to warm up and sleep in the unheated room. Despite the nuisance of an extra trip before spending the evenings with the Caddys, those hikes, following the countless animal and human trails winding among the hillocks and dunes, were for me the highlight of that period.

It was a strange situation for us all: three mature and active people more or less hanging around together for no known reason. We had no jobs, having tried to get them without success. This in itself was strange, since Peter and I were both qualified and had never before had any difficulty finding employment. Despite the fact that we had gone through hells and bits of heaven together, we certainly did not stay together there for any personal reasons. At first we felt sure that we would be spending just the winter there and would return to the hotel when it reopened at Easter. It was only the reassurance of our inner guidance that kept us in the situation.

The first few months we spent repairing the caravan. Following Sheena's training to do everything with love, to the glory of God and as perfectly as possible, we sanded every unevenness from the surfaces of the trailer inside and out, and achieved impeccable results. After all, there was no lack of time to pressure us into botched jobs. A mobile library supplied us with books. I read autobiographies and murder stories. Peter, who had always had a wish to start his own garden but had very little opportunity for practical gardening, mainly read gardening books. We were isolated from everyone and everything, our only contacts with the outside world being a trip to nearby Forres when Peter and I collected our weekly unemployment benefits. Although we kept in touch with what was happening in the world through television and newscasts, our vital interest was in changing human consciousness, which the news rarely mentioned. In any case, changing consciousness was an individual task; we were getting on with it as best we could.

Our continuing inner work had different focuses at different times. In the early Findhorn days, and with another like-minded friend, Lena, who joined us in the spring, we spent a great deal of time telepathically contacting the Network of Light. Briefly, this network was like a communication grid on subtle levels, covering the world in triangular patterns. The 'stations', usually manned by a group of spiritually dedicated people, existed in most countries throughout the world. This network had been charted by an American friend of ours through telepathy, and we ourselves linked with it telepathically, sometimes receiving from these groups, sometimes broadcasting to them, and always linking the whole together in love. We also had telepathic communication with beings known in certain esoteric circles as the Masters of the Seven Rays. Basically, these Masters are highly developed humans who have accepted responsibility to aid humanity. Focusing on these beings as I knew them, I would get on their wavelengths, there being a distinctly different energy feel about each one. I was developing the faculty to attune to and distinguish subtle vibrations.

Easter came and Peter had received no offer to resume the management of the hotel. Since it seemed that we were stuck there for another year, I ordered an annex from local builders for my accommodation. To supplement our food supply and to fulfil his wish to have a garden next to the trailer, Peter began to cultivate a small patch of ground, six by eleven feet, on which he grew a quick crop of radishes and lettuce. More time passed without jobs materialising, while he continued the cultivation of more ground around the trailer. This was no easy task on sand dunes in which only gorse and coarse grass grew. Underneath there were fine crops of pebbles very suitable for soakaways, but not for gardens. Peter cut off the top layer, then Eileen and I, occasionally helped by the boys, picked out the pebbles for about a foot down. Then Peter laid the top turf in the hole, upside down, and we shovelled the sand back, mixing in any bits of available compost. Then Peter planted vegetables, or sowed seeds. The many gardening books he read were a mixed blessing, with one book suggesting one method and the next advocating a different procedure — and none of them written for garden vegetables in sand dunes in northern Scotland. Our days began to centre around the garden, and we pursued our gardening with the same kind of care and perfection that we had learned to put into everything. It was hard physical work, often dreary, but being outdoors made it enjoyable to me.

In one of my meditations early in May I received an interesting, new directive from within:

> *To those who have an insight into life, everything has meaning. For example, there is a spiritual meaning behind the constant blowing of the wind, in spite of any unpleasant results it may bring.*
>
> *The forces of Nature are something to be felt into, to be reached out to. . . . One of the jobs for you as my free child is to sense the Nature forces such as the wind, to perceive its essence and purpose for me, and to be positive and harmonise with that essence. It will not be as difficult as you immediately imagine because the beings of the forces . . . will be glad to feel a friendly power. All forces are to be felt into, even the sun, the moon, the sea, the trees, the very grass. All are part of my life. All is one life.*

46

I thoroughly approved of this suggestion, thinking it would be a good excuse for time spent on walks or lying in the sun. I have always felt best alone in Nature. To me, lying in the sun with as much skin exposed as possible is not only a sensual delight but almost a spiritual experience. I feel blissfully spaced out, as if absorbing some sort of wholeness, and not even exposure to the tropical sun in Panama cured me of the feeling. But when I showed this guidance to Peter, he took it to mean that I was to feel into the forces of Nature to give him information about the garden. Next morning I received:

Yes, you can cooperate in the garden. Begin by thinking about the nature spirits, the higher overlighting nature spirits, and tune into them. That will be so unusual as to draw their interest here. They will be overjoyed to find some members of the human race eager for their help. This is the first step.

By the higher nature spirits I mean the spirits of differing physical forms such as clouds, rain, vegetables. The smaller individual nature spirits are under their jurisdiction. In the new world to come these realms will be open to humans — or I should say, humans will be open to them. Just be open and seek into the glorious realms of Nature with sympathy and understanding, knowing that these beings are of the Light, willing to help but suspicious of humans and on the lookout for the false. Keep with me and they will not find it, and you will all build towards the new.

I was left with a sinking feeling in my stomach. I felt totally incapable; how could I attune to beings about which I knew nothing? These seemed to be neither the fairies of children's literature nor the creatures of myth. Anyway, I was afraid that I might be under some illusion. I stalled, yet I knew from experience that I couldn't forever disregard an inner directive. While I was filled with all these disbeliefs and questions, Peter had none at all. His background in positive thinking trained him to admit no doubts. He had his faith affirmed by following Eileen's guidance for years, and he immediately accepted all guidance from us in complete faith. Peter, all action himself, expected the same of us. When I told him I couldn't do what my guidance had suggested, he simply replied, in his usual supportive, though forceful manner: 'Nonsense, of course you can.' This too probably put me off, since I have always responded better to requests than to commands.

With a sincere desire to increase our own firmness in action, Peter had, in fact, shared with Eileen, Lena and me a series of lectures that had been part of his training. Included in these was the exercise of repeating the phrase 'I am Power.' I had considerable trouble with this exercise at first, because I don't like the thought of power with its implications of force. I would not repeat the phrase, although I had no compunction about repeating, 'I am Love.' Then, on analysing myself, I concluded that the word 'power' was not the culprit, but the word 'I'. I had been thinking of the limited human personality called Dorothy as the 'I', as the power, instead of the unlimited God-essence of Dorothy. When I changed my identification, I could happily repeat that phrase. I was going through this series again, and on repeating 'I am Power' one day, some weeks after the earlier guidance to contact the forces of Nature, I slipped into a stream of power. I became so identified with power that I felt I could do anything, even attune to the essence of the spirits behind Nature, as had been requested of me, for I as God-essence could be one with the essence of any part of creation. Vegetables had been mentioned in my guidance, and as Peter was interested in receiving guidance related to the garden, I decided to choose the garden pea, since it was growing in our garden and I had known it since childhood. I had a clear sense of what the plant was in terms of its colour, shape, flower and taste, and moreover I loved eating peas. Drawing on my familiarity with and fondness for peas, I imagined and focused on their essence, or inner spirit. The response was surprisingly immediate:

I can speak to you, human. I am entirely directed by my work, which is set out and moulded and which I merely bring to fruition, yet you have come straight to my awareness. My work is clear before me: to bring the force fields

48

into manifestation regardless of obstacles, of which there
are many on this man-infested world ... While the vege-
table kingdom holds no grudge against those it feeds, man
takes what he can as a matter of course, giving no thanks,
which makes us strangely hostile.

What I would tell you is that as we forge ahead, never de-
viating from our course for one moment's thought, feeling
or action, so could you. Humans generally don't seem to
know where they are going, or why. If they did, what
powerhouses they would be! If they were on a straight
course, how we could cooperate with them ! I have put my
meaning across and bid you farewell.

Although unclear as to what it would mean, cooperation
with the spirits of Nature was an acceptable idea, since to me
cooperation was and is the way to relate. When I showed the
typed message to Peter, he composed a list of questions for me
to ask the spirits of the various vegetables, since he had been
facing a number of challenges.

Thus began a day-by-day unfoldment in communication
with the forces behind Nature. Peter, of course, would try to
find a reason for a plant's malfunction himself, but when he
found none or did not know what to do, he would give me
questions. Then I would attune to the spirit of the particular
vegetable for the answer. Having done it once, I couldn't use the
excuse that it was an impossible feat. In fact I now realise that
my own or anyone else's belief in our limitation is the greatest
block to achievement. So circumstances, using Peter as their
able instrument, kept forcing me to turn to the Nature forces.

For instance, we had two sowings of dwarf beans; the first
lot didn't come up, while the second lot seemed promising. The
spirit essence of dwarf beans told me that the first lot had been
sown too deeply and before the soil had sufficient nutrition, but
that the other was fine and was being worked on by them. The
spinach sprouted so well that Peter asked if it was too thick. I
received:

If you want strong natural growth of the leaf, the plants

will have to be wider apart than they are at the moment. By leaving them as they are, you will get overall as much bulk in the leaves, perhaps a little tenderer but with not as strong a life force. I, of course, like to see plants given full scope, but the choice is up to you.

Even at this early stage, no laws were laid down and human freedom of choice was integral to the cooperation. Whatever we asked, I received an answer of some sort, sometimes merely 'yes' or 'no', and sometimes an explanation. For example, we were told, on request, when to water each plant, where to put in new ones, which needed liquid manure, etc. For the first couple of years, until we became familiar with this unfamiliar view of garden growth, Peter had frequent questions. However, he acted at once on suggestions given. Otherwise, I believe, the cooperation would not have continued.

As to who these Nature beings were, I quickly realised that each was not the spirit of the individual plant but was the 'overlighting' being of the species. I discovered that the being behind the garden pea held in its consciousness the archetypal design of all pea plants throughout the world, and looked after their welfare. Obviously such beings must function in more than our three dimensions, but my previous telepathic contact had made this concept familiar. A slight acquaintance with Theosophical literature, together with my inner promptings and the tremendous purity, joy and praise which these beings emanated, led me to conclude that they were some type of angel. As the word angel had a very restricted and stereotyped image in my mind, contrary to the impression of lightness, freedom and formlessness given by these beings, I decided, generally, to call them 'devas', a Sanscrit word meaning 'shining one'. The word was no doubt often used in India, but it was not hackneyed or conventional to my mind.

The Pea Deva was the first to come into my awareness. The second which my inner guidance suggested I should contact was a being overlighting that particular geographical area. I called it the Landscape Angel. I was told it would answer general questions concerning the soil at first, and later it would act as envoy for the whole angelic world. The Landscape Angel was very keen on compost, indicating that man had to play his part in this cooperation and that we couldn't expect them to do all the work, especially to grow vegetables in unnourishing sand. This Angel gave fairly detailed instructions on compost making, when to turn the compost, whether it should be mixed with the soil or laid on top as a mulch. Imperceptibly, the Landscape Angel gave us a more holistic approach to the garden, helping us to see it as part of the larger environment. We began to see the soil as part of a living organism and the plants as links with their environment, a focus of energy integrated and interacting with its surroundings. As my inner guidance said:

> *As you read and try to understand that book* (**Agriculture,** by Rudolph Steiner), *you come across what are called cosmic influences on the Earth emanating from the various planets. Think of that planet as a living Being, and also as the forces being relayed by Beings and being received by Beings. There is no such thing as dead matter. Everything is living and everything has a place in my one life; and that life force is more than what you call magnetism. It is an influence consciously wielded on the higher levels. You are simply surrounded by life; you are a life force moving among other life forces. As you recognise this and open up to them, you draw near to them and become one with them, and work with them in my purposes.*

The Landscape Angel said that since Peter, through me, had voiced the need for the ingredients necessary to make the soil live, he would be shown these ingredients as we did not have the money to buy them. Indeed he was: grass cuttings from the trailer park; soot from an ancient dump used by local chimney-sweeps; seaweed from the shore; and horse manure that we collected with buckets and spades from a field, to the puzzlement of both horses and passers-by. Once we obtained a biodynamic preparation for compost. All of us, including the children, went through the ritual of mixing it in a big vat, going round and round giving it the prescribed number of turns. It was fun and

51

hard work; in fact this whole period was one of healthy, hard work for us all.

*It was the reality
of the garden growth
that brought home to us the reality of the devas.
Out of this grew a new way of gardening,
and a deeper understanding of life as a whole.
We were learning the importance
of cooperation, not only
with Nature but amongst ourselves as well.*

Chapter 5

Adventures in Understanding

Within a few days of my initial recognition of the Landscape Angel, it began to give us, in addition to the gardening directions, information of a more subtle kind, information new to us at the time. It said that the radiations put out by every gardener contribute to the growth of the garden and that these emotional and mental forces are transmuted by the nature forces and can add to plant growth. Certain people stimulate plant growth, others depress it and even draw from the plant. When our forces are consciously focused towards adding to plant health, this produces a still greater effect. Like children, gardens need tender loving care. In turn, children and happiness are very good for plants. Human affirmative thought protects and feeds plants, as it does all of life. Our separative thought jars Nature patterns. Flavour is improved in vegetables grown in a harmonious atmosphere. Our thanks and appreciation unite us with the life of whatever we are thankful for and appreciative of, making a compatible blend of forces to help development on various levels, including the physical. As positive thoughts and emotions influence the plant, the resulting higher quality food that we eat influences us positively — an ascending spiral. Weak plants can be strengthened by thinking of them as strong.

The application of these principles was not easy and was

part of a long process. For instance, when I saw a sickly plant I registered it mentally as sickly, and it was far more difficult to think of it as healthy than to think of a healthy plant as being healthy! This seems too obvious for words, but recognising and changing our habit of judging by appearances is the beginning of creative living. Here again the angels helped, by suggesting other approaches, for example, that we think of plants in terms of light, as vital patterns of energy, which I assume is the way they see plants. Much later, Kirlian photographs gave me a glimpse of what they might mean.

We were told that our differing energies were good for the garden and therefore as many people as possible should work in it — except, of course, if we were so wrapped up in our own problems that we emanated only dispiriting and enfeebling radiations. The thought of my personal hang-ups affecting innocents like plants and animals was an extra incentive to turn to the higher part of my nature. Gradually, but oh so slowly, I became more aware of my own state and more selective as to what part of myself I lived with and expressed.

The powerful effect of our thoughts and feelings was well illustrated by the growth of a small chestnut tree, planted just when we were beginning to expand into a group. There was something jaunty and endearing about this little tree which caught the imagination of us all. Because it was situated where we frequently passed, we would often stop to admire it, both silently and audibly. The more it thrived, the more we expressed our admiration. It grew a really fantastic amount, far more than would a normal chestnut tree, so much that it overshadowed and crowded its neighbours. Peter decided to move it to a location where it would have more space. The move was a group effort that must have looked very funny. The top of the tree was braced on the back of a station wagon, while the well-wrapped roots were carried shakily on a wheelbarrow. In between, a crowd of us tried to support it in some fashion as we gingerly proceeded to the new destination. The Chestnut Tree Deva thanked me for our joint efforts and care, and said that one of the reasons why this particular tree had flourished so well was because of the love and appreciation it had received. If the tree were to thrive equally in the new site, then we would have to go out of our way to give it as much attention. We did, at least for a while, and the tree is still flourishing, although not to the extent of those early years. According to the devas, gratitude and appreciation have enormous effects, making great swelling movements which complete the circle of life.

Besides the Plant Devas, other non-human beings shared our life. The land surrounding our little garden was full of moles. Their favourite food, earthworms, began to be produced in large luscious quantities in our compost and hence in the garden. The moles swooped in, riddling our plots with tunnels and depositing great heaps of pebbles in our neat rows of vegetables. To make matters worse, plants began to die as the tunnelling left roots stranded in air. Peter, no doubt thinking that moles would be easier to contact than vegetables, simply asked me to do something about it. As usual, I felt quite incapable. The idea came to me to make a mental fence around the garden to keep moles out — anything to avoid having to contact the animals — and my inner guidance and the Landscape Angel both encouraged me in this. Feeling very foolish, I would sneak out surreptitiously at dusk and circle the garden, envisaging a fence of light as a barrier to moles and stopping to contemplate clouds if anyone came near.

But mole-proof fences weren't exactly cooperation with moles. I knew I would have to try to contact them. I was encouraged by a book, **Kinship with All Life.** In it the author, Allen Boone, tells how he came to realise that a certain dog had pre-knowledge of his movements. Changing his attitude from that of teacher to that of learner, he developed a communication with the higher intelligence of the dog and later with that of other animals and insects. My own instructions on contacting natural forces had been to feel into their essence. Moles were unknown to me, except soft-hearted Mole in **Wind in the Willows,** so it was difficult to imagine their essence. That was the reason, perhaps, that the level of mole intelligence which I contacted was not the light angelic sphere. In my mind's eye appeared a gloomy underground cavern with a very large — larger than I — hostile mole confronting me. Taken aback, I stammered out my story of how we were trying to grow a garden, how it was our source of food, how we were even cooperating with Nature forces. I said that I myself would never hurt a mole, though I could only speak for myself. The moles were spoiling our garden. Please, would he arrange for them to go elsewhere? No reaction. Just hostility. I repeated myself, metaphorically backing away in the process, and left as soon as I politely could.

The next day there were no new mole pebble mounds, nor the following day. I relaxed, uneasily. In a week's time Peter appeared to remind me to do something about moles — another mound had appeared. I repeated my plea to the mole. There was another week's respite before Peter appeared again. As I thought I was getting nowhere with that unfriendly mole, even though I considered its attitude the result of human crusades against the animals, I decided to concentrate on the fence. Turning within, I was told:

> My child, the mole fence as constructed is right . . . but it is the mortar, your belief, which crumbles. Part of you expects it not to hold up, and therefore of course it doesn't hold up. Your belief has to grow so strong that not only will it hold up against any attack but will be creative in itself. . . .

After that I sneaked around the garden area again, building fences, but moles were beginning to haunt me and become a great burden. Mole mounds must have appeared again, for a week later I recorded this message:

> You felt resentful that the mole broke into the garden last night while you were asleep, which you felt was not your fault as you had given it over to me for that period. My child, you were completely casual in that giving over. It was merely a passing thought and you put no conviction into your request. Therefore, it was not effective. How often have you been told that there is no sitting still in

*my life, but a continual reaching forward? This is being
brought home to you constantly with the mole, until at
times you wish you could shoot the thing, or you think it
is all a pack of nonsense, or unfair. But I tell you to go on
and on. Let moles be a challenge instead of a burden.*

Stirring stuff for a skit, but it was far from funny at the
time. My guidance during the next few days included more talk
about lackadaisical fence building, about learning to put all of
myself into a project instead of getting by with part of myself. I
was informed that I had never been told that it would be easy
to build a fence, particularly because of the runways into the
garden which the moles follow blindly.

*You feel that you are being led on like a donkey with a
carrot. Of course, you do not know the way in these
realms, and you have to be led or you would stay still.
Be grateful that you are learning, and have to turn ever
closer to me.*

I was learning, ungratefully, it seemed to me at the time, only
that my power of sustained positive thought was feeble. Yet
even that can be a necessary step to changing one's approach.
Not until much later did it occur to me that perhaps I was also
being shown, because of my decision to concentrate on building
walls, that walls of any kind, even if well built, may not be the
answer to problems. At any rate, evidence of moles in the garden grew less and less, then vanished, and after that first summer
no moles entered. This was a tremendous relief to me, for I
could not have faced another such mole season. Not that I considered that I had been instrumental in the vanishing of the
moles; I just thought that something else had probably turned
up and was grateful for that 'something else'. However, two se-
quels pointed to other conclusions.

The first came about seven years later, when we had grown
into a community. We acquired some adjoining land which had
always been full of moles. The team of gardeners came to ask
me to clear this new area of the animals. I genuinely felt that it

was their problem now, not mine, for I was working only in the office. Also, contact with different areas of consciousness is open to us all, and these gardeners were very sympathetic to animal life. Therefore, I merely shared my experiences with them and suggested that they try the same sort of cooperative approach, following their own feelings. They did, and the moles disappeared in record time.

The second episode occurred about the same time, when I had moved into a caravan on the outskirts of our expanded community area. One November day a mole mound of stones appeared on my lawn. As there was nothing else in the area that he could undermine, I concentrated on this one mole to let him know that he could rampage in my lawn during the winter, but come spring, please would he go? He seemed to take me literally; he tore around that lawn. I was forever picking up piles of pebbles that he unearthed, both amused and annoyed at his intense activity and the trouble it was causing me, and at myself for using the word 'rampage'. When spring came I steeled myself to ask him to go, for I was rather afraid that he wouldn't. But his response was immediate — straight into the garden of another group member! On asking him to head the other way out of our area, I got the impression both of humour and 'Well, why didn't you say so in the first place?' He went out directly. I could see his trail going past my caravan out to a field. It was a good lesson on the need to be specific and accurate in my communications. But what was tremendously significant to me was that the response on both occasions was too immediate to be coincidental. Finally I was convinced of the validity of cooperation between humans and wild animals. The mole seemed to want to prove that it worked. I believe that animal intelligences are very aware that a new cooperation with man can develop, and that they go out of their way to show their awareness.

For several years the garden was the recipient of all our time and energy. Peter acted instantly on the advice given by the angels, and we soon had a fine supply of vegetables for Eileen to cook. Many different varieties were introduced, including some that none of us had come across before. With the constant addition of compost, the sand began to turn into soil. It was very intensive gardening. Soon all the land around the trailer was under cultivation, as well as the hill of our hollow, which we terraced. We planted herbs and experimented with them in the daily salad. We began a small orchard of apples and gooseberries. Before each apple tree was put in, we removed over twenty-five barrowloads of sand and stones, replacing them with an equal amount of sand and compost. Fortunately the gooseberry bushes needed fewer barrowloads exchanged. We handled, literally, tons of sand.

Berries grew well in the long summer daylight hours and Peter planted them everywhere. Some sturdy blackberries acted as shelter belts as well as producing bushels of fruit. Raspberries and strawberries were our delight; we even reached the point of being unable to eat any more of them, an achievement we had never dreamed possible. We were vegetarians by choice and necessity. An unforeseen joy was the flavour of the vegetables; we had forgotten how delectable a taste came from vegetables grown without chemical fertilisers.

We began to have sufficient surpluses to sell to other people in the caravan park. Our produce was good and attracted still more people. Local market gardeners thought so highly of our young plants that they even began to buy them from us. With the money we could buy more seeds, plants, frames or shrubs for a hedge.

We were very pleased with and grateful for the fine produce. In our ignorance, we had no way of evaluating it. When we paid a visit to Cawdor Castle, whose large walled gardens had been well tended by a team of professional gardeners for centuries and were open to the public once a year, we saw that our vegetables and fruit were healthier than theirs. We began to realise that this cooperative work with the devas was more than proving itself.

At Peter's request the County Horticultural Adviser came to analyse the soil. He pronounced it, like all soil in the district, deficient in certain ingredients, but took samples for testing. However, the soil analysis showed no deficiencies; the soil was perfectly balanced. The Horticultural Adviser was amazed and just could not understand it. The devas could, saying:

*We knew that this garden would confound the experts, be-
cause it is not like other gardens. Yes, we can and do draw
to ourselves what is needed in our work from the everlasting
life substance. This process is speeded up when the material
we need is available to us in a form easier for us to use,
that is, when it has already been converted. This, of course,
is where your cooperation in putting materials into the soil
makes all the difference to the plants.*

*This process is also easier for us when your creative
power is flowing to the land, when what is coming from
you is of the highest. Man counteracts our work not only
by the poisons he purposefully puts forth, but also by the
many ways in which he breaks cosmic law in his selfish-
ness. When all is more or less in line, as in this garden, our
creation forges ahead not only unimpeded but accelerated.*

As we did not consider that the Horticultural Adviser
would approve of or believe in angelic help, we told him nothing
of it. But he was so impressed with the soil analysis and the
growth of the plants that he asked Peter to take part in a gardening discussion on BBC radio. On this program Peter
attributed the success of the garden to good composting
methods and hard work; he thought that Scottish gardeners
would not readily take to the idea of angelic help either.

In 1966 we made the acquaintance of R. Ogilvie Crombie,
a cultured elderly gentleman from Edinburgh with a scientific
background and broad interests. Almost immediately Ogilvie,
for the first time in his life, began experiencing a relationship
with Nature forces on a different level of the Nature kingdom.
He saw and communicated with little beings such as fauns,
fairies and elves, and the god Pan. His experiences added
another aspect to our cooperation with Nature, perhaps best
described as more concrete and particular. For instance, from
the devas I never had any impression of opposition. If human
actions were too repugnant to them, they would simply with-
draw. Ogilvie's little beings were much more 'human' and could
get angry. Therefore, when we did something inimical to them,
we learned more quickly and specifically from their reactions.

And many normal gardening practices inhibit Nature's ways.

In addition to the contribution from the nature spirits to practical gardening, Ogilvie's attitude was a great support to me. We did not have to talk; we both felt the same way about gardening. Indeed, I often needed at least his moral support, because Peter, who after all was playing the role of man in our cooperation with the Nature forces, had the normal human attitude of treating plants as objects to be manipulated rather than as relevant parts of a greater whole.

One novel idea that Ogilvie gleaned from his contacts was that every garden should have a wild area which humans left alone and undisturbed for the nature spirits. We immediately allocated a small hilly part of our plot which had already been planted with various small conifers. Later, when one of these trees began to encroach on a neighbouring gooseberry bush, Peter wanted to trim it back. Having already learned from experience to be careful about cutting trees and shrubs, he hesitated and sought advice from Ogilvie. The guidance said that Peter had enough facts to decide on his own. To be on the safe side for a change, he left the tree alone, and the nature spirits said he would not regret this. When we had a bumper crop of blackcurrants that season, while elsewhere the blackcurrant crops failed miserably, Peter wondered if we had been compensated in this way.

Cooperation apart, we had not been aware of even obvious ecological connections. One year we had a plague of wasps building nests chiefly on rafters above doorways. Thinking only of the constant traffic and the people who might get stung, we kept removing these seminal colonies until the queen wasps were forced to go elsewhere. Later on that year we had another plague, this time of caterpillars on the cabbages. A knowledgeable visitor, on seeing the caterpillars, asked, 'Have you no wasps?' Evidently wasps were the natural predators of one cycle in the life of the cabbage moth. We were learning the hard way, like other people all over the world, about the interconnection of life. What the devas were saying became increasingly authentic to us. Peter had fewer and fewer questions to ask of the devas as he gained experience in following their advice. I con-

63

tinued to contact the angel of each new addition to the garden, quite an extensive job when we expanded and added many varieties of flowers.

In 1966 we, and Peter particularly, broke out of our hermitlike existence and began to travel in Britain. We met people, told them about ourselves and our garden, and they began to visit us at Findhorn. All were attracted by the vitality of the plants and the vibrant color of the flowers, and those with gardening experience were astonished and puzzled that from that soil and climate should come such fine specimens. Some visitors, attracted by our way of life, joined us, and our group began to grow. Not until we had a visitor, Sir George Trevelyan, who was conversant both with spiritual matters and the soil, did we mention to someone outside the group about our cooperation with the spirits of Nature. Sir George accepted our explanation, urged us to write about our experiment, and contributed a foreword himself in which, after praising the garden and saying that more than good composting must have been involved, he wrote:

> The ancients, of course, accepted the kingdom of nature spirits without question as a fact of direct vision and experience. The organs of perception of the supersensible world have atrophied in modern man as part of the price to be paid for the evolving of the analytical scientific mind. The nature spirits may be just as real as they ever were, though not to be perceived except by those who can redevelop the faculty to see and experience them. Perhaps the phenomenon with which we are now concerned is simply one of the many examples of a breakthrough from higher planes leading to new possibilities of creative cooperation.
>
> As I see it, the implications are vast. The picture the devas give is that, from their viewpoint, the world situation is critical. The world of nature spirits is sick of the way man is treating the life forces. The devas and elementals are working with God's law in plant growth. Man is continually violating it. There is real likelihood that they may even turn their back on man, whom they sometimes

consider to be a parasite on Earth. This could mean a withdrawal of life force from the plant forms, with obviously devastating results.

Yet their wish is to work in cooperation with man, who has been given a divine task of tending the Earth. For generations man has ignored them and even denied their existence. Now a group of individuals consciously invite them into their garden. They are literally demonstrating that the desert can blossom as the rose. They also show the astonishing pace at which this can be brought about. If this can be done so quickly at Findhorn, it can be done in the Sahara. If enough men could really begin to use this cooperation consciously, food could be grown in quantity on the most infertile areas.

If Caddy's group have done it, many others can do so too. Wherever we are, we can invoke our devas, who doubtless are instantly in touch with those on the same wavelength anywhere else.

The contact will not necessarily bring a scientific knowledge, though this may follow. It will work in the immediate intuition of the gardener so that his hunches may guide him to the right, though perhaps unorthodox, action. This is well demonstrated in Caddy's case, and many others who will acknowledge and love the nature spirits may, even if they are in any way sensitive, find that their gardens begin to grow and respond as never before, and that they are led with surer intuition to do the right thing in planting and tending.

The possibility of cooperation with the devas should be investigated seriously. The time has come when this can be spoken of more openly. The phenomenon of a group of amateurs doing this forces it into our attention. Many people are now ready to understand, and that enough should understand and act on it is possibly of critical importance in the present world situation.

The response to this first booklet proved that many people did understand, for many wrote to thank us for our work with the devas and nature spirits, and to say that it confirmed their own similar experiences. More visitors came to see us, and some stayed. A sanctuary and an office had already been built and a printing machine acquired; now a large community centre with sufficient kitchen facilities to cater for two hundred people was constructed, following guidance, although the group numbered under twenty-five. More horticultural experts came, including Professor Lindsay Robb, a Soil Association consultant. With a background of agriculture, conservation and nutrition, he had served as consultant for the United Nations and other organisations in various posts around the world. He too was amazed at the garden, and he wrote:

> The vigour, health and bloom of the plants in this garden at midwinter on land which is almost barren powdery sand cannot be explained by the moderate dressings of compost, nor indeed by the application of any known cultural methods of organic husbandry. There are other factors, and they are vital ones. Living as this group is living, on the land, by the land and for the love of the land, is the practical expression of a philosophy which could be the supreme form of wisdom — and freedom.

Other gardening experts wrote as enthusiastically. None could find a rational explanation for the results in the Findhorn garden, because the methods used were not rational. But co-operation with the forces behind Nature does not mean that we throw aside gardening as practised down the centuries, or that Findhorn is unique. For instance, biodynamic gardening is based on the seership and cooperation with Nature developed by Rudolf Steiner, on principles laid down by that great sage. The cooperation at Findhorn was not based simply on following mandates laid down by the angels, who were very careful not to make rules or regulations, but on the principle that man is a co-creator and his own innate creativity is the best gardener. We were urged to experiment, we were urged to add another dimension to our thinking and feeling, and to find our answers from within ourselves.

It was the reality of the garden growth that brought home to us the reality of the devas. Out of this grew a new way of gardening, and a deeper understanding of life as a whole. We were learning the first principles of group work — the importance of cooperation, not only with Nature, but amongst ourselves as well. There was the interaction between what the Nature forces were saying through Ogilvie and me, Peter's application of this to the garden, and Eileen's guidance encouraging me and confirming Peter's actions. There was the interaction of our personalities; and above all, there was the individual desire of each one of us to move with the highest aspects of ourselves. Though occasional tension arose, we were learning how to combine our own practical understandings into one creative whole. As Peter became a gardener through practice, the devas began to relate more and more as educators. Just as they had taught us to see subtler aspects of Nature, they taught us how to live in touch with subtler aspects of our own beings.

Of course it is a fact,
but what do facts
matter?

Hazrat Inayat Khan

Chapter 6

The Angelic Realm

What are the angels? Obviously they represent a kind of life, a kind of perspective of the universe and a kind of dimension of beingness which is not subject to proof, as we understand proof through scientific and technological conditioning. Earlier cultures seemed to require no proof of the existence of these beings and took them for granted. Perhaps our forebears were simply superstitious, or perhaps they had some way of experiencing these beings and thereby accepting their reality.

The **Encyclopaedia Britannica** defines angels as 'a term used in the Christian religion to describe a being endowed with intellect and free will, specifically distinct from and superior to man, but essentially inferior to God.' The Encyclopaedia goes on to say that they are variously called messengers, sons of God, spirits, holy ones, hosts of heaven; that their number is myriad myriads; that their functions include praising God, attending upon His throne, executing His commands, protecting the faithful. In Isaiah the attendants upon the divine throne are called seraphim and are described as having a human figure with six wings. Cherubim, the guardians of paradise, in the visions of Ezekial have four wings and four faces. The **New Testament** confirms and supplements the **Old Testament** teachings, and theologians commonly divide the angels into nine orders or choirs differing in rank, these being, from the highest rank down: seraphim, cherubim, thrones, dominations, virtues, powers, principalities, archangels, angels. Probably the best known story is of the angel Gabriel being sent by God to Mary to announce the birth of Jesus.

Through my Christian background and Christian paintings, I had naturally come across these beings, though they had no reality or meaning for me. Only now do some of the many words about them come to life, such as when I read that seraphim is derived from a Hebrew word meaning 'to burn' or 'to flame with life'. However, in London I had come across a small book about fairies by E. L. Gardner, which contained photographs of fairies supposedly taken by two girls in Yorkshire together with an explanation of these beings as part of the natural processes of growth. As, child-like, I had always wanted to believe in fairies and since the explanations made some sense to me, I had accepted the ideas as valid, particularly as my husband had said that of course they were true. Later **Kingdom of the Gods** by Geoffrey Hodson, with its many beautiful color plates of drawings of angels, devas, sylphs and gods, considerably enlarged my views. I gleaned the impression of a vast hierarchy of supraphysical beings acting as agents for God, directing the laws and processes of Nature on and beyond this Earth. Although parts of the book meant nothing to me, the concepts satisfied something deep within. Therefore, when I contacted the overlighting being of a garden pea, to my mind it belonged to this chain of life. From then on I was on my own. I had to piece together various fragments to make a picture of these dimensions as I encountered them.

In addition to the difficulty of a realm which transcends our normal experience, it is also difficult to describe it with words invented for life within time and space. For instance, I used the word speedy as an adjective for the devas, to convey the meaning of everywhere-present-at-one-time-in-movement. Or I would grasp one point enough to sink my teeth into it, only to find that in the process I had ignored many other aspects.

I could list many interesting facts about the angels I have

picked up over the years but, as Inayat Khan said about re-incarnation, 'Of course it is a fact, but what do facts matter?' They matter only as they relate to our life, only as we can apply them. In the interplay with the garden many things became alive. For instance, the devas said that what we saw as a heavy inert clod of earth was to them alive with light and life. That non-fact became our fact later on when we heard fascinating talks from Donald Wilson of the Soil Association about the myriad, teeming, minute life contained in one square inch of soil.

Because the devas wanted us humans to cease thinking in terms of limited categories and to expand into a greater wholeness, they resisted any attempt to be departmentalised or classified. Thus I find it difficult to categorise them. On initial acquaintance, I had immediately mentally labelled them as members of the angelic chain of life ranging from the little beings of folk lore (the elementals) through to a vast hierarchy of beings up to a cosmos beyond human imagination. My own guidance said that the overlighting spirits of Nature had jurisdiction over the little nature spirits, which I assumed were the elementals of medieval myth who work with and enliven earth, water, fire and air. The devas have alluded to such a hierarchy, always underscoring that we must not cage them in *our* understanding. Indeed, if what we can understand with the rational mind is the apex of our knowledge, then analysis is of prime importance. But when higher faculties like intuition enter, classification must either serve willingly or sink newborn intuition with its weight.

The devas are the builders of our world. Embodiments of creative intelligence, they wield or transmute what we might call energy (vibrating waves or particles in patterns) into increasingly more 'physical' structures (including emotional and mental structures) and finally into what we call matter (which is pattern in space). They build vehicles for the expression of life on all levels: mineral, vegetable, animal, human and suprahuman. As builders of life, obviously they have long inhabited our planet. In fact they formed planetary life, and as such are Lords of Involution and Evolution, moulding increasingly finer, more precise, more sensitive vehicles for the expression of consciousness.

As builders in energy, they find the bricks for that building in unlikely places. I have already mentioned that they converted necessary ingredients for the soil 'out of the air', that they converted our appreciation for the chestnut tree into growth for the tree, that they used our positive thoughts to strengthen sickly plants. In their view, all life is interacting force. They say humans are builders too, transmitters of force, but very ignorant ones at present.

In their capacities as builders, the angels were part of the history of the Earth before those latecomers, humanity. In a sense they are our parents, having in the infinite, intricate resources and processes of Nature produced bodies for us, too. They are immutably linked with Earth, yet are beyond it in their cosmic roles. They, too, are learning and changing, and they say devic and human destinies merge.

They hold the archetypal patterns of our planet in a sort of inner energy stream of divinity. Though ever conscious of this divinity, they are not, on the level that I contact, initiators of new patterns. Even in the garden this became evident; they opted out of planning and left that to the gardener. They were eager to help in any plan Peter suggested: when he asked whether to try one of two alternatives, they might propose trying both. To me it seems that their relationship to choice is conditioned by two factors: first, as beings who flow with energy fields, they are not choosers, nor possessors of free will; second, in their capacity of educators, they want us to develop our own abilities and be dependent on no one. They said it was not their work to change patterns, that they work with and within conditions, while man can change conditions.

The first characteristic which became apparent to me about the angels of the plants was their wonderful feeling of lightness, in the sense of being free and unburdened. Perhaps this is not surprising in beings unconfined to physical bodies. On the other hand, they are responsible for the physical development of plants, which, goodness knows, have a hard time keeping their shape while providing food for most of life.

The second characteristic which I registered was that these

74

beings knew what I was thinking. Yes, said my inner guidance, they live in a sphere of immediacy of knowledge. Whatever they must know for their work is immediately available to them. They knew what was in my mind and so I didn't have to spend a long time phrasing questions for them. They also know our motives; we cannot fool them. Theirs is not the selective, garnered wisdom of the human race; it is an ever-fresh knowing, a pure intelligence, which includes a certain pre-knowledge, such as knowing the broad lines of the processes of evolution.

The devas are immensely powerful. As controllers of natural systems, as agents for creation's patterns, one could almost call them all-powerful. Rarely did they show this side of themselves to me, for I was uncomfortable with it. However, because of their attitude to power, it sat lightly on their shoulders; they talked of the beautiful use of power (see Wormwood Deva, page 113). In due course, when humans are ready, the devas can share more on this subject, especially as they say that we are potentially unlimited.

As far as feeling goes, the devas are a constant source of joy and upliftment. G. A. Gaskell's Dictionary of All Scriptures and Myths defines Devas, 'Shining Ones', as 'Exalted Intelligences of Truth, Wisdom and Love, on the higher planes. These operate from the buddhic (wisdom principle) and higher mental planes in furthering the process of evolution. They are concerned with the higher emotions, and are attracted by aspirations from below . . .' These higher emotions or qualities are immediately evident when contacting any level of the angelic world, and to come into the presence of such joy, love, purity, lightness or peace (the fruits of the spirit in St. Paul's definition) is to feel completely refreshed and new, yet deeply at home. These qualities, these emotional expanses weave into all aspects of the angelic world, making their work a play, a dancing ecstasy, a consummate artistry, a pure delight, a peace beyond understanding. In the messages I tried to convey something of the varied, sensitive beauty and fun of the world of angels, but no words can convey it.

As for the form of the angels, I do not see any, although occasionally I have had an impression of colour or pattern. They

Landscape Angel drawing by Brian Nobbs

76

say that they are not bound by form, that their form changes as they move, partaking of the qualities of the realms they transit. Because they are not visible to our normal sight and because they are so changeable and moving, compared to our ideas of form they are formless. I believe that there are times, when they wish to communicate with humans, that they take on a consistent shape for the purpose of being intelligible to us — after all, most of us would not consider communicating with a moving pattern. Applying this principle, the smaller nature spirits, i.e. goblins, elves, fairies, are sometimes seen by children dressed in the traditional fashions of the Middle Ages. This style of clothing is a carry over from that period when some humans were still generally close enough to Nature to relate to the fairy world.

I asked various and silly questions about the angelic world, such as 'Do you eat food, say nectar and ambrosia' or 'Do you ever attend lectures?' These were either answered ('Our food is energy radiation'; 'We do not attend lectures') or put into proper perspective by the angels laughing at me and merrily vanishing from consciousness. I did have impressions of the Cabbage Deva as being motherly, with her babies hanging around her skirts, or of a fire deva as very masculine; but on the whole the devas seemed relatively formless and sexless.

Then one of our group, Brian, felt inspired to draw these beings, and produced a version of the Landscape Angel. Though I liked the drawing, it upset me greatly. Not only was there a definite outline but it was obviously masculine, and to me the Landscape Angel was both masculine and feminine. However, on consulting the angel, it said that it was delighted with Brian's effort, that his view was bound to be different from mine as different consciousnesses tune into different qualities. To prove its point, the Landscape Angel thereupon demonstrated to me an aspect of itself that I had not encountered before; very calm, powerful, almost cold traits. It went on to say that as Brian and I both knew that its form was almost incidental, because so changing, to put something on paper with rather insubstantial lines was one way of bringing the reality of the devic world to human awareness, and thus helping to bring about cooperation. As cooperation is essential, the devas were deeply satisfied to see these pictures developing.

Formless or not, the devas were certainly individuals, each uniquely different. Otherwise no one would be able to contact them nor feel the essence of each. Yet, though fully individual, they did not mind losing their individuality and merging into the whole. The whole, of which they were a part, was of over-riding importance; the oneness of all life was a consciousness in which they happily had their being. When conveying some idea to me, perhaps one deva would speak, or perhaps a host of them; it didn't matter to them and soon ceased to puzzle me. It was my first experience of true group functioning.

I do not pretend to understand the complexities of angelic building methods as described in esoteric traditions. These expound on seed atoms of the various vehicles of life, which become increasingly complex until, in man, there are physical, emotional, mental, intuitional and higher components. As far as the most familiar body, the physical, is concerned, esoteric lore talks of an etheric duplicate, a more subtle rendition of the physical. This etheric body has force centres known as chakras, the etheric counterparts of various organs and glands, and holds the pattern for the physical. The devas that work on these levels construct and adjust, according to individual patterns, the delicate mechanisms of consciousness.

The devas hold the archetypal pattern of all form, not just human form. Paul, in the New Testament, says 'Through faith we understand that the worlds were framed by the word of God, so that things which are seen were not made of things which do appear.' (Heb. 11:3) The Weeping Willow Deva gave me an understanding of this by inviting me far into their worlds, almost to a point which contains all life.

Here is concentrated stillness and from here radiate plans and patterns. From here I reach out a long arm to each willow in the world, containing it in the stillness and bathing it with radiance. It becomes a distinct entity on its own, but is nevertheless part of the invisible consciousness which I am. From my point of stillness great ripples of energy go forth.

I wondered whether the deva, at that point, was aware of other devas, and it answered:

Yes, I am aware of those like me similarly engaged, but in the point itself the pattern is exclusive as it ever emanates out. Yes, I am aware of being contained in the greater Stillness. I am sharing with you this aspect of ourselves, this holy place of creation. Breathe softly and do not disturb the delicate force lines here at source.

Of course, the angel did not refer exactly to physical breathing; my trips to their realms were in consciousness.

The deva went on to say that, like humans, it had many levels of awareness, and it then took me to the level of the tree in the garden so that I could feel the pattern there. I encountered blurred outlines, and was told that this was the result of the transplanting that the tree had undergone recently, that its lines of force had been weakened. The deva asked us to give love to the tree to help it overcome its traumatic experience. The deva further explained that it had shown me the indomitable, focused side of angelic nature, the holding of the pattern from the centre out to the farthest specimen. To these patterns the devas are bound. At the same time they are the freest beings in creation.

On a later occasion the Apple Deva talked of the process of creation, of the Word being made flesh:

From the seed idea a pattern of force issues from the centre, passed on by silent ranks of angels, silent and still because the idea is too unformed and unfixed to endure any but the most exacting care. Down and out it comes, growing in strength and size, becoming brighter in pattern until eventually, still in the care of the outmost great angel, it scintillates and sounds. Its force field is steady and brilliant. Then the pattern is passed to the makers of form, the elementals, who come and give themselves to clothe that pattern. Remember, this is a process, that the pattern is everywhere apparent in the ethers held by the angels

*and made manifest by the energy of the elements through
the ministrations of the elementals at the appropriate
opportunity, and then appearing to you in time and place
in beauty of blossom and succulence of fruit.*

The Landscape Angel once seemed to be juggling forces
into the area with 'hands', and said that the devas work in
mantras, in movements, which produce sound and make a
pattern, and work up to a certain pitch. Their movements
endow their areas with certain qualities of life.

A shrub deva talked of joy as the impetus to the direction
of force, as the nature of life itself, the lifestream of Nature.

*We fly on the wings of joy, for we could not manipulate
forces if we were weighted down like humans. We start
plants off by whirling forces into activity, and the joy in
us has a constant movement which we pass on in our work.
What fun it is to hold each little atom in its pattern!*

To them, the formative field for manifestation is abounding joy,
so it is not surprising that joy is everpresent when one becomes
aware of the angels. They express their joy in praise of life, as
well as in the creation of it, and this is the truth behind medieval
paintings of angels singing praises to the Lord.

Another way in which the devas function is in abandon-
ment to the moment, in full concentration and oneness with
current energies. As the Landscape Angel mentioned, they use
all conditions, making the best of unexpected human actions.

The Landscape Angel explained its function as a director
of streams of light to the Earth, not just for vegetable growth
but for many purposes, such as relaying energies from stars,
always balancing and refining them. Such angels are conscious
power stations. Because of the deep awareness of divinity in all
that they do, the forces they handle are not impersonal wavelengths but carry a source of upliftment, of beauty, of wonder.
This is another way by which they play their part in the upward
spiralling of life.

Devic life has a constant sense of service, some of it

directed to man. Great Beings of Fire from the Sun pour out highly energising radiations to help uplift the Earth, but do it infinitely slowly in order not to harm us. At the same time they accomplish other things, for they are part of all they meet in a multidimensional way. Devas pass on life. They are workers creating form for developing consciousness, morphologists unveiling to humanity ever greater realms and wider levels of creation. There *are* Healing Angels, Guardian Angels, Angels of Art, Sun Angels, Angels of Love.

About a month after my first contact with the Pea Deva, for some reason the Landscape Angel took upon inself the task of broadening my mind. Suddenly, but rather formally, as would befit a British Landscape Angel, it introduced me to an Angel of Sound. As usual, I made a record in words:

My sounds are everywhere. You may think that the wind rustling through the leaves, for example, is what produces sound, but this is only the means used for my effects. It is the same with your voices; the sound builders in my realms help each human to develop his own creative sound. There is no separated life. All is vibration, all is life. Each range of manifestation is assisted by life, by beings. I merely bring this to your notice to enlarge your vision. When you hear a skylark now, you can think not only of that beautiful sound as produced by the bird and by its and our Maker, but by the angels and beings of sound who have helped to produce that song. All these aspects of life are to become more real to you, and so I compose these notes, to add to the whole. I will come again.

This was fascinating to me. Without saying much, this angel raised a host of ideas in my mind. We have rudimentary knowledge of what are doubtless immense new worlds to conquer, and in a week's time I tried to find out more by attuning to the vibrational level of this angel. I converged on beings who identified themselves as of the Sound Angel branch attending to Light, the Sun's emissaries on Earth to make sure that light is able to be revealed by life, through the medium of sound. This was unintelligible to me and they sympathised, saying:

> No wonder, human minds are not thinking on this subject. You think of photosynthesis, but see no connection with sound. Although our realms are not measured by your science, look up the process of photosynthesis.

They continued to expound on individual plant notes and individual human notes, which have very potent effects. In the plant it attracts life substance through the nature spirits. In the human who has harmonised all parts of his being the note is immensely powerful. In a sense, sound and light are the same; light and life shine through any being which sounds its own note. And the sound comes first. As I didn't see what these angels had to do with this process, they explained that, like tuning forks, the individual notes resonate in the various plants or beings, and that the note changes with growth. This process, which was not clear to me at the time, I later understood.

The next message from the Sound Angels mentioned that theirs is a group work, because sound is so interacting, and that humans too would be working in groups for more completeness. Later (still in 1963), the Sound Angels commented on how my Earth-trained mind was inclined to make them a race apart, forgetting that all is sound or vibration, forgetting that angels are not limited in form. Thus they tried to expand my understanding, and when they saw that I was still uncomprehending, said:

> Yes, you will discover that what we mean by sound and what you mean by sound is quite different. Our conception is broader than yours, of course, because you are limited to what you hear through your ears, although you know in theory that all is sound and that life is movement producing sound. To us this is not theory but life itself.

Then they gave me helpful advice about not despairing because of my lack of understanding.

82

If there are Angels of Sound, are there then Angels of Silence? When I asked, the Landscape Angel was an intermediary for me as I was unable to go far enough into the silence, and said that the Deva of Silence unobtrusively straddles the universe, coming to have real meaning for us when our consciousness is closer to Source. Silence is a living, healing force for human seekers, and evidently even for plants, as the great Angels of Silence go deep into the roots of each plant to make it aware that, whatever buffeting it may receive, all is well.

This was rather mind-boggling. Personally I was far more interested in colour than in sound or silence, and would have preferred to contact Angels of Colour. I now believe that my very interest, which had led me to explore the subject and form definite ideas, caused a barrier. I had to be content to receive information now and then, like the following from the Landscape Angel:.

The plant devas, like others of the devic world who deal with specific patterns, have a definite and pronounced colour pattern in themselves, being the embodiment of these energies in our world. The colours that they wield are extremely clear and definite, for we hold to our purposes with a concentration rarely known among humans, who are distracted by their emotions and their passing thoughts. The colours, of course, are of a brilliance which your solid paints can only suggest. Movement, the constant flow of energy, is another characteristic of our world which can barely be suggested in paint.

To concentrate on our colours would be an overwhelming experience, for you are accustomed to the muted tints of Earth. We deal in what would be a riot of colour to you, and we find our stability and rest in a dazzling whiteness of light, rather than in the darkness, sleep and cessation of activity that is peace to you. Like you, the plants have their periods of rest. Not so with us. Clear colour is an inseparable part of us. You would feel light-headed in our flashing colour world, and would also be upset by the lack of fixed form.

Some day it would be a treat to explore the dimensions of Colour Angels, but at Findhorn I was discovering further branches of the Devas of Nature, after my God-voice reminded me that all creation was embodied and suggested that I harken to the 'mythological' being of the wind. The wind, which would blast the garden and depress both Eileen and Peter, exhilarated me, made me want to be disembodied and to fly. I had some difficulty in attuning to the Spirit of the Wind, for I didn't know whether to blend with a soft zephyr, a rollicking gale, or a furious cyclone. And then, maybe there was something even beyond these. I was told:

> *Come deeper, below thought, and, as in the still centre of a cyclone, imagine our evolution on this Earth — millions of years of patterns of behaviour, as your bodies are the results of millions of years of evolving patterns. Imagine the effect of an atom bomb on our volatile medium after aeons of orderly existence. Yet we are intimate with humans, to whom we bring the breath of life from the Creator. Consciousness of the oneness of life is what is important. Like all life, we are not what we may seem, and if you will listen, we will always communicate some of its aspects. Nothing is static, particularly in our realm of air, so do not try to pin us down, but let us try to understand one another. Until next time, we are off with the wind!*

That being I could relate to, even carelessly connect with the four, fat-cheeked fellows who puff from the corners of many maps, but I was in for a shock. To my great surprise, after five years of almost daily contact with beings of the angelic world, I realised with joy, excitement and awe that the mythological gods of Greece were members of the angelic world. This recognition was another instance of the truth of the oneness of all life — a leavening of the coded virtues of the Old Testament with the grace and beauty of the pagan world. I understood that the allegory of Psyche, the soul, who after many testings eventually married Cupid, love, and became a goddess, was the same story as that of a Christian following Jesus' greatest commandment: to love and thereby become a Christed being. With fresh eyes I saw the reality in a previous intuition of the old gods stirring and coming to life. I saw that the aid offered by the devas had always been available to man and could be traced in myth and legend. I understood the appropriateness of the fact that the two great Mystery Teachings of Greece came from the two *earth* gods, Demeter and Dionysus, who kept suffering pain — for pleasure and pain, good and evil, are teachers. Many correspondences and understandings leapt to my mind.

I started to strain for more interconnections, and was told from within to let things develop from an inner knowing rather than from the outer. For instance, I had been puzzled why the gods of Olympus did not behave at all laudably, while the devas were beyond reproach. I was told that the explanation of this discrepancy was that every age interprets life according to its own preconceptions and motives, projecting its own emotional imbalances on reality.

Another area of the angelic world came to life after this revelation, one which had been alluded to before but which I had not taken seriously because it seemed so improbable. I tuned into the quality of serenity one day and an intelligent, communicating being came to my consciousness. She said:

> *The One All-Being mentioned the gifts of the spirit, and then you did not wonder by what means these gifts are poured forth. I bring the gifts of serenity, peace, and poise. I enter your being with my being; we correspond and lo, you are serene. I and my brothers and sisters come from the realms of the gods which you call pagan. Yet in fact we more truly serve the Lord of All than do humans, for we stray not in our fidelity, nor turn our backs on our god-selves.*

So Serenity, Wisdom, Love and other qualities are beings, intelligent forces that take on life in various realms! Doubtless they are the Virtues, ranked fifth in the hierarchy of Christian angelology, as well as being ancient goddesses and gods with different names in different cultures.

My understanding of their embodiment is not that they, the archetypal patterns, are separated individual persons, any more than God is a separate individual person — or that humans, for that matter, are simply separated, individual persons, for we too have other dimensions. Everything functions in levels beyond the physical. The intelligence that we are and the intelligence that the angels are, the intelligence in eveything, is unique yet universal, for the God-principle exists in all life. One definition of the devas would be the intelligent principle of growth, whether that growth be physical, emotional or mental. Through our intelligent principle we humans can perceive intelligent principles elsewhere, though our interacting and changing perceptions vary with our awareness. We understand nothing unless we have, in some way, the same vibrational experience. We cannot truly understand the taste of an apple until we taste it, through our taste buds. The old saw that we can only see someone's fault because it is also our own still holds truth. We cannot understand jealousy, or joy, or sarcasm, or creativity unless we experience these emotions or these ideas through our emotional and mental equipment. Such equipment has devic builders, vibrational manifestors. The vehicles through which we experience have been developed by pure intelligence through the agency of the devic builders — and we are part deva, we have angelic selves. We are also constantly creating on the emotional and mental levels.

By mentioning that angels are builders of emotional vehicles through which we experience and express jealousy, for example, I am not suggesting that there are jealousy devas. As I have said, the angels use the qualities of their realm for constructive, holistic purposes; they have no choice. Jealousy is a human expression. We humans can choose to express the universal building bricks, the qualities, either positively or negatively, and jealousy is merely a fragmented, or polar-opposite expression of love, trust and gratitude. In our freedom of expression we are potentially greater than the angels, who create only according to the will of the whole. There is no good or evil in their realm. We are the creators of good and evil; we have eaten of the fruit of the tree of the knowledge of good and evil. We can harness atomic power, which is neither good nor evil, and if we create a waste disposal problem, we can also create the solution to that problem. In my experience, restrictive separative energies are the result of man's choosing to create for the good of the part, not the whole, and through these choices we learn and move. From the vibrational world of our angelic selves we help build our vehicles and create on all levels, according to how we choose to use our unique gift of free will. To me, the gods of evil are manmade, which does not make them any the less powerful or dangerous to those who share the level where evil has reality.

There should be a clearer distinction made in that confused area of human thought and feeling often called psychic. What is normally called psychic does not occur in the realm of the soul, the psyche, but in the realm of human emotional and mental projections, the astral realm. We create thought-forms out of thought energy which form real patterns in the mental realm. We read a story of honest George Washington and we add our bit of mind stuff to the image of honest George, and the world mental image of an honest Washington grows according to the strength of our thought. Our children tune into the same image, and may or may not strengthen the pattern. Then someone may write a book disproving the story that little George said he could not lie, and presenting another image of the man so strongly that we the public create yet another mental image of Washington which is real for us at the time. This sort of thing is even more easily done with distant historical images, and I am sure that the pallid Jesus of my childhod was of human construction, that Nero or Atilla the Hun had some virtues. We create meaningful images like that of Uncle Sam, or a flag that we must salute. In the subtle astral and emotional levels, so close to the 'Virtues', where human and soul goodness interact, our wishful thinking can create Masters or angels coming to tell us that we have a special job to do, and deceive the very elect (if any). The line between illusion and reality, madness and genius, is very shifty. In this time of moving into the intuitional realm and new discoveries, it is hard to know whether a quark or an angel is a quirk. Since on one occasion, out of deep, unrecognised desires, I had called my own hopeful projections the voice of God, I was wary and suspicious. But I could not deny beings that came to my consciousness when I was attuned to the soul level.

A Sun Being (could it be Apollo?) illumined my consciousness with a message:

> *Child of Light, seek the light because you are light. I speak from the Sun, and always you hear my call. I touch you with my fingers from millions of miles away, and yet as my fingers are part of me here, so are you. As the great God who conceived us all is always here and always there, lives and breathes and grows. I touch myriad other lives, and they too are part of us.*

A further message on the unity of all life came later, blazoned forth by another Sun being:

> *We reach out and intelligently draw your planet to the one scheme of things. Unity is being showered upon your world as never before, and we reach and serve on many levels in this same purpose. We would give you a glimpse of our beneficence, embracing all, and consciously directed at mankind.*

There is no end to these beings. The Spirit of Night, evidently used to being maligned by humans, talked of itself:

> *Humans commune with me in unconscious sleep, but rarely do it consciously. Yet what a great gift I bring to you all! Were it not for night time oblivion, which is a rhythm of your worldly life, you would be conscious of your ever present problems, and that would be too much altogether for you. Renewal, conscious and unconscious, comes when I come, and with it much that you take for*

granted. That does not matter: it is sufficient we all fit in the plan of things. Nevertheless, I find a certain joy in having a listening ear. Part of you still does not really believe in me, but the part that does thereby contributes to the oneness of life. All that you think of is life and intelligence, for we are all a drop in the ocean which is the life of God — and you are not the first to think of the Spirit of Night, even if we have been relegated to mythology and poetry. What a superior concept is the old idea of a spirit, compared to present day acceptance of measurable facts; influences, perhaps, but remote, dry and uninteresting!

I love all life, and with my cloak I cover up each little yesterday for each of you. In me you find rest, and when you leave me you go with new life, life whose wrinkles I have ironed out while you were in my care. I am the inviting nothingness of darkness into which you must float in faith, unknowingly, from which you return renewed. Thank God for me, for sleep, for life, and respect more the processes of which you are a part. Let us all give thanks.

From this you will see that I was still of two minds about the reality of some of these beings. It was not easy for me to go against normality when I could prove nothing to myself or anyone else in a pragmatic way. It is not easy for our souls or for our intuition to surface in a materialistic world. Nevertheless, I continued to have experiences with beings of other qualities, like Perfection and Fun, and beings of the elements, of air, of rain, of water. Fire was evidently a tricky element; I was told to come to the God within when considering fire:

The Fire Beings are mighty, princely and mysterious, not quite blended with man — did not Prometheus bring fire to man only to be perpetually banished by the gods? Yet fire is here, in the volcano, in you. Don't play with fire; grow in stature to become one with it and then its constructive and destructive aspects are one with me. Its great volatile

power, its cosmic flame, will kindle consciousness might-
ily. Nothing else is so effective. Bow low before the Lords
of Flame, purify yourself and rise with them to great un-
daunted heights, but with me. It is the way of the razor's
edge for any who deviate. The intensity of the power is
tremendous. Remain as my small child and you are as
large as the Sun.

A year later I did get in touch with some Lords of Flame from the Sun, who greeted us Sun lovers and talked of the Sun as the spiritual centre of this solar system and of their own function as controllers of the fierce forces linking life. To my questions, they said that man, too, would learn their secrets in due course.

Let your dominion be over yourself,
and let your expanding
consciousness see
God's life in
all things.

Cosmic Angel of Stone

Chapter 7

The
Living
Universe

The beach at Findhorn has marvellous pebbles. Like most people, after a walk across the moors and along the shore, I almost always returned to my trailer with pockets heavy with stones that took my fancy. In fact, under and around most trailers were little piles of pebbles dumped by departing visitors when they considered weight limitations. One day I was admiring a translucent pink pebble gathered on the moor, when it occurred to me that I had never contacted a deva of the mineral kingdom. I decided to try, deducing that as minerals were a lower form of life than plants, the deva would be a primitive simple type of intelligence. To my astonishment I found myself in rapport with the mightiest Being of my experience, one that stretched out and out to infinity. This cosmic Angel of Stone confirmed that it was concerned with mineral life in various stages throughout the expanses of the universe, and continued:

> *Nature is full of paradox, in that as you seek contact with what you consider a lower form of life, you in fact contact a more universal being. The mind of man codifies and formulates, which is within its right and purpose, but forgets that all is one, that God is in all, and that basic*

substance, seemingly most devoid of sensitive consciousness, is held in its state of existence by its opposite, a vast consciousness, too vast for you to do more than sense its fringes and know that it extends beyond your present imagination. You realise too that dense matter is influenced in its make-up by stellar energies.

It was the beauty of this particular stone which drew you to me. Beauty is of God, beauty is working out in all levels. Consciousness of beauty brings you into oneness, into any part of the universe. You are contained in it just as I seem to contain universes within myself. The more you appreciate beauty, the more you are linked universally. It is good to seek it on high levels, for then your consciousness is expanded.

You feel right now that you can only look at every pebble with deepest reverence and worship, because it is part of my vastness. We are glad that in this way you have been shown a very little of the glory of God. The glory of God is everywhere, stretching from the farthest reaches of the universes to the little grain of sand, one and the same thing, held in eternal love and timeless with life.

Yes, of course it would be good to attune to me if you work with stone. Reverence all life, emulate my patience, unfold the mysteries of God and even of pebbles. Do it as a learner of life, a revealer. Let your dominion be over yourself, and let your expanding consciousness see God's life in all things, where indeed it is, and, as you have learned, in the most surprising things. The colour and sparkle of a stone is wonderful, but more wonderful is consciousness which has brought about and brings about those outer manifestations and grows cosmically. We are all part of one life, no higher or lower. Praise God forever in the vastness of all life.

For quite a while after that insight I would go to the beach, lie on the hard uncomfortable stones as a worshipper, and link in imagination with great and simple glories—hoping no one would see me. Also I had been given another look at my preconceived and limiting ideas. It seemed to me that, because the mineral world is so rigid, so unable to express sensitive keen life, only the loftiest, the most selfless, close-to-God being would accept mineral embodiment. And such embodiment was a matter of acceptance; that Cosmic Angel had the power of choice among its endless faculties.

Nature conglomerates, like mountains or a bay, have devic presences. The Findhorn Bay deva said that tidal land had a good and cleansing influence. The deva gave an impression of timeless love, always changing, always brooding over the ebbs and flows of its life in an eternal optimistic patience.

Mountains have distinctive devas. I first touched the edges of them in the West Highlands by Loch Maree, and received the impression of great age and deeprootedness:

> *Our consciousness is so deep in the Earth, so used to channelling through rock, that we are almost as divorced from our higher selves as are humans. We are deep down, firm and constantly overshadowing our environment, attached to it and paying heed to little else. We do not mind if you try to translate our consciousness in your words — what is one passing human in eternity? We steady and maintain. We are the great maintainers of the world, the strength of the Earth itself continually translating forces up and down, the pores of the Earth breathing, and I, one entity commanding here. There are many of us. We go on forever. I know man changes and alters the countryside. That is only at our feet and he has not altered us. We are of the Earth itself. We are before and after man. You say that it is up to man to lift even us. Well, that remains to be seen. We wish him luck and we get on with it, and withdraw to do just that.*

An adjacent mountain, Slioch, continued in a view not so disdainful of humanity:

> *We too are older than time, with a softer, more spreading influence than our neighbour. Whatever the weather,*

whatever happens, we spread the energies out into the sur-
round, out from the depth of the Earth and out from the
heavens. With our head in the mists, our arms in the loch,
and feet deep down, what we do is beyond the comprehen-
sion of man, too timeless for his little mind to grasp, be-
longing to the world of creation with no beginning and no
end. It is purely beneficent, however hard we may seem.
Softness is hardness worn down; hardness comes first in
this world. This we know and so we stay eternal, forever
working for the Creator of all.

Later, when I came to America I stayed on a ranch on the
slopes of Mount Lassen, said to be the only active volcano in
the continental United States. I climbed the easy ascent and, at
the peak, tuned into the essence of the mountain. Again, I had
the impression of great and ancient depths, with a hint of new
and available-to-humans, transmuting energy, the potency of
which I do not think comes across in what I wrote down at the
time from the deva:

I seem in the depths, invisible, and I shake off with my
elbow the accumulated refuse of the ages, for now is the
time for a transmutation of it. Yes, if such as you can be-
come clear and sparkling, with minds full of light in all
situations and places, you transmute too, and we are one
in our function. We would gladly let you do it your way,
for that lightens the processes as nothing else can, and we
willingly lend you our fire, which you are anyway.
You ask about devastation. There will be some devas-
tation in California, regardless, but that need not worry
you; it is always so. Yes, some is humanly preventable,
literally by humans channelling more light, fire. The more
you can kindle the better.
You ask how that will affect us. We will remain what we
are, but more attuned to the rest of our brethren, more
part of the world whole, sending out more cosmic fire, for
we will be linked up more consciously with our fellows in
other worlds. I stir, as I always do, but chained still by

patterns that I accepted aeons ago. You humans are the flower of those patterns and it is your turn to use fire to change Earth, as your consciousness burns outwards and inwards . . .

Later the Angel of Mt. Lassen explained more of what it meant by its fire energy by calling itself an Awakener, purposeful and mighty, aware of its responsibilities to man and using whatever opportunities arose. It was a very potent and creative energy.

I was privileged to see another type of angel grow. This was the angel of our group, the Spirit of Findhorn. Any unit or group of units which is distinct enough to form an identity, whether it be a man, a bay, a farm, a nation or a planet, has an ensouling presence. As usual, it was the Landscape Angel who first mentioned that a being was forming from the unity of our thoughts and feelings, of our garden, of all that we were doing. This being was under the care of a neighbouring deva, and was rapidly developing its own peculiar beauty. We were told that we gave it strength from the depth and dedication of our activities as we aimed for perfection. When I asked if it had a baby form, the Landscape Angel gave me an impression of an adult still unformed and asleep, a sort of Sleeping Beauty figure. It said that this new deva drew substance from all of us, from all that comprised the place, yet it had a life of its own and that I would have to get used to the vague overlapping boundaries of the ephemeral inner worlds. Of course what came to my consciousness here, as in all things, were symbols which had meaning to me; someone else might have understood immaturity by some other symbol such as an unjoined circle.

My first hint of an Angel of Findhorn came when we had been in the caravan park for nine months, and for some years I received glimpses of its growth via the Landscape Angel. The second time the Landscape Angel said that the deva had a certain difficulty in forming because there was plenty of higher energy to use but little variety available in the physical geography of our tiny plot of land. Next I was told that it was gathering life from all of us in a new unity with mankind (no doubt because of our recognition of it). It was still nebulous, though growing phenomenally fast; we were in a sense part of its body and it would act also as a bridge with us for others of the devic world. I received an impression of closed eyes, of reposeful hands, and of great length. The Landscape Angel added, 'Definite warmth directed to it will speed up the process and quicken its life.'

Later the Landscape Angel told me that the deva was growing in harmony with the garden growth and that, though I sensed open eyes and head movement, it was not yet coherent enough for me to contact. I thought it interesting to have the Landscape Angel remark that all devic knowledge would soon be open to this new deva, but that we humans still generally limit our reservoir of knowledge although eventually we would also tune into much wider ranges of knowing. When I asked if the rhythm of a year was necessary for full growth, the answer was yes.

I forgot about this deva, and it was not until several years later that I attuned to a rather masculine Spirit of Findhorn and received:

> *I take my stand with my brothers, tall and one in essence. Immensely vigorous and vital am I, with a role that reaches to the four corners of the Earth and beyond. We all rejoice among ourselves in these realms in which, with the help of you all, has been born and grown to fulfilment one such as I, a prototype of cooperative activity. I have been planned from near the Godhead, and given sustenance by both the devic and human world.*
>
> *Do not form a clear concept of me and so keep me in limitation. The image you have of me is of immensely vital young manhood, which is a small and current view. I have many parts to play and much to do, and we shall do it together.*
>
> *Now I go from your consciousness, but I am in you and you are in me, different yet one. I am the Spirit of a place, yet how much more. You are limited human beings, but*

*you are gods in the making. We are one because we have all
been given life.*

My next understanding of this process I put into the following words:

*From an unawakened godling I have grown to a stature
reaching up to the highest, for the spirit of a place does
not depend on the physical size of the land. Many factors
come into my makeup, but now my greatest characteristic
is height — up, up and up. I can mean many things to various
souls, but all would be directed in a straight line to the
heights. That straight line leads to the heart of all things,
to God, to be found high up, or deep within, in the Sun itself,
whatever way your consciousness is tuned. I would
lift you out of yourself into your Self; for that purpose
was I brought into being.*

Although the community only vaguely acknowledged this
angel, we did have a lot of fun with it, producing a song with an
endless number of verses, in which we all joined on Fun Nights.
Fortunately, I can only remember the first line of the chorus:
'Angel of Findhorn, open your eyes.'

I believe the angels of countries or races have as one role the
furthering of consciousness of all in their care, and in a sense
each brings certain vibratory activities as the goals or focal points
for their nation. These angels are perhaps the Principalities of
Christian angelology, and our national symbols, like the
American Eagle, the British Lion or the Russian Bear, are frail
representations of their potencies.

When I returned to a disunited Canada in 1976, I contacted
the overlighting angel for its view of the country's situation.
This led to my exploring my roots, which I had thought nonexistent
or irrelevant as I considered myself a citizen of the
world, and to my giving a series of exploratory workshops on
national identity and the part it had to play in our makeup, if
any. In Canada, national identity was a vital subject and our
workshops were a transformative experience for those who

99

attended, helping us realise how narrow our outlooks had been and how different is the view of a country's purpose from the soul level.

*   *   *

I have already told the story of my contact with a level of mole consciousness. Before the moles had proved that they were cooperating, I was forced by circumstances to try to communicate with the angelic presence of yet another member of the animal kingdom, one for which I felt both fear and hatred: rats. I had the usual cultural antipathy to these vermin. Attracted by the food in the compost heaps at a time when we were beginning to expand and put our attention on other things than good compost making, they were multiplying. This didn't affect me until a family of them moved into a cosy corner in the railway sleepers that upheld my annex, and their nocturnal scratchings kept me awake. I would thump the floor vigorously from my bed, and hear brief skeltering noises followed by silence. The silence would last until I was just about to fall asleep, when renewed scratchings under my bed would jolt me to full attention. A repeat performance would follow: a thump and shout, silence, time to get really dozy, scamperings, wide awakeness. After three nights of this I was bleary eyed, useless and ready to try anything, even to talk to rats. So, rising to as loving and clear a state as possible, I attuned to rat-essence and explained that human beings, at least this one, needed sleep, that I couldn't function without sleep and that, if they must make a noise, please would they make it during the day. I said that I was asking their help as fellow beings, and could reward them in no way, although of course I myself would not harm them. In short, I explained my predicament and asked for help. There was silence and I slept. The next night there were some perfunctory scratching noises and I again appealed to the good nature of the rats: silence, blessed silence.

After that I heard no more rat noises. Although naturally grateful, I didn't really believe that my pleadings had influenced their behavior; I thought that probably they had found better quarters and had moved away in the normal course of events. I just forgot the incident. I remained in the annex four more years until all of us, the Caddys and myself, moved into separate caravans. Naturally our old accommodation was needed for group members and one of them, Eddie, moved into the annex. In the morning he came to me, wild eyed, saying that rats had kept him awake all night and had been trying to get at him. I could hardly believe the astonishing fact that these creatures, perhaps through generations, had, at my request, either left that place or kept quiet for four years. I immediately experienced an about-face in my attitude to rats: fear and horror turned into an admiring love and friendship. The animals were proliferating at that time and I would catch glimpses of them when walking past the compost heap; after that revelation we seemed to wink at each other in mutual fun and secrecy.

Naturally, I related my new-born love of rats to Eddie and others, and suggested that they try the methods that had worked for me. I was not successful in arousing in them a similar love. Eddie, who had a strong dramatic flair, said that his nights were terrifying, and kept insisting that the rats were eating their way into the room to get at him. He stayed there a very short time. Janet, who was in charge of sprouting wheat for community salads (a dietary addition which the rats evidently found particularly delicious) would alternate between an attitude of 'Dear Ratty' (she also had read Wind in the Willows) and 'the brutes are going to win, I know they are.' In the end we all failed, for, in spite of my entreaties, poison was put down and the rats killed, for the ostensible reason that the community feared a visit from the Sanitary Inspector. I was not strong enough either to cancel out or change the negative attitude of other people to rats. I gather rats are a recurring though not perennial problem at Findhorn and probably will remain one until all concerned can be united in a holistic approach to them. Obviously, even the thought of cooperating with such a universally condemned creature is difficult, quite unlike the thought of cooperating with a beautiful flower. But I know it can be done, and that rats are gentlemen.

Later I read about a very similar, more successful experience, in Allen Boone's The Language of Silence. He was visiting a family plagued with pack rats. After hearing of all the terrible things the rats were doing, he explained to the family that everything that appears as reality is in fact in one's own consciousness, and that their expectation and belief that the trade rats would enter their house and carry away valuable things had brought about its own fulfilment. They were simply experiencing the operation of the law of expectation-and-fulfilment in action, overlooking the fact that nothing can be created in their experience that does not reflect the content of their thoughts. He convinced the family of this, and they decided to try an experiment.

> They would all stop the viciously bad thinking they had been doing about the trade rats and try to never again harm them, mentally or physically. Instead, they would look only for the best in them and expect only the best from them. Thus did they establish the law of universal love in their hearts and minds, and set it vibrating in the direction of the trade rats. Then, to their fascinated delight, the magic rebound happened. Echoing back from the trade rats came their invisible as well as visible best. As a result, every trade rat disappeared, and permanently so, from the publisher's lovely mountain estate. And what had brought it all about, they discovered, was simply a change in concepts.

Perhaps the strangest deva of all was brought to my consciousness in 1969. The group at Findhorn had expanded to the extent of acquiring our first printing machine, a second-hand offset litho machine that had stood long and neglected in a local government office in Elgin. We did not know how to run this machine, and I therefore attended a short course in Edinburgh for this purpose. On my return I tried to put my new knowledge into practice with the help of Pete, a group member who loved machines of any sort and who was our maintenance expert at that time. What with the neglected state of the machine and our inexperience, we learned by trial and error, and every trial seemed to bring a new error as we attempted to print our first publication, Parts I and II of the initial *Findhorn Garden* book. We were learning the hardest possible way, on paper masters (originals from which copies are made) beautifully and carefully typed by me with even right and left hand margins. The slightest spot meant a retyping, perhaps when we were only ten copies short of requirements — and we did not know then how to obtain durable metal masters. We became slaves to that machine, trying to anticipate its every move, and every day learning a different lesson with 'George', as we called it, who was always one jump ahead of us.

Then one day Pete and I independently realised that George did not have a relationship only with us, but that it reacted to other people entering its room. It reacted violently to one individual in particular, spewing ink or paper in all directions whenever that person came near. Pete and I speculated on the possibility of machine devas. I consulted the Landscape Angel and was told that indeed there were devic beings of machines, who were some sort of cross between humans and devas and who had human likes and dislikes. Evidently George had developed a human sulkiness due to neglect and was very touchy. After introducing me to a machine deva, from which I received impressions of darkness, a new departure in devic realms, the Landscape Angel explained:

> *This patch of darkness, along with a certain inflexibility which is foreign in our makeup, is but a measure, on the inner planes, of the outer limitations imposed by the mind of man.*
>
> *No, it is best at the moment that I act as spokesman for these devas, because what you love in us is our flexibility, our freedom from the mind, our service to God, and the machine devas are a different breed. Look at it this way: before there is any manifestation on what you call material levels, there is first the idea in higher substance. Man, coming to his estate as creator, is learning, as a child learns in building with toy bricks, a certain control of the higher patterns which are the seed energy of matter. He unconsciously builds in higher energy a prototype of a machine pattern, for example, and because his consciousness is*

limited and he is only concerned with part, the seed energy or deva of that machine has limitations. Instantaneously and automatically we, the divine energy, are there to imbue this poor creation with more of ourselves, to educate it, to coax it to its immediate purpose.

So machine spirits function in our world and yet not in our world entirely, being children, shall we say, who will grow into adulthood as man grows in stature. But talk to them as to a fully grown citizen of our world, as you would to us, for their true essence is God also, and the more you recognise that, ignoring the limitations, the more will the God-essence be drawn out. It might even be good practice for you, as in seeking only the pure God-essence in these devas you will likewise seek only the pure God-essence in other humans!

I have come across other people with the same strange kink of finding it easier to see divinity in a flower, an animal or a machine than in their fellow humans! Yet I knew that the Landscape Angel was being very generous in saying that the reason why it acted as an intermediary between a machine deva and myself was due to my love of devic lightness, when in fact I actually had no love for machines. Even when grateful for the work they did, I had always considered their straight lines and dull colours ugly and ungraceful. The Landscape Angel confirmed my admission, adding:

The Machine Deva is larger to you now and very imminent, but the time for direct contact is not quite yet. Your contact with us, which has been guided and is no chance happening, has a certain purity, and all is not yet clear between you and machines. Feel no guilt; this is not a thing just of the personality and you are merely a representative of mankind in this matter. Much has to be worked out in many ways between man and the various representatives of our kingdom.

Two months after my initial realisation that there was

such a thing as a machine deva, I had some slight contact with it and shook hands, metaphorically, feeling as I did so the best of wills on both sides. But the Landscape Angel said that it would continue to act as an intermediary, as I was still inclined to forget that machines had a life of their own, and that direct contact depended upon my attitude towards them. I was further educated in attitude when the devas said:

Do not talk down to a machine. On the material level the machine may seem to you to be nuts, bolts and other bits of unconscious metal, but the higher counterpart is one with us, all-knowing and all-serving. So raise your consciousness in your dealings with machines, as well as attending to their material needs, and then you are more truly addressing the whole being. This practice of course applies to anything, humans as well. It is easy for you to see the limited outward manifestation and forget that behind it is a divine spark. Life is one and it is well to remember that. I know you cannot soar and feel freedom with a machine deva as you can with nature devas, and there is no need to. You know the purpose of that machine; make full use of it in cooperation. Do it all to the glory of God, and all will fall into place.

Pete and I gradually became more aware of the machine as a living being, and even tried to change our view of it by changing its name from the common 'George' to the more elegant 'Gadriel'. We certainly got better results. Solutions to problems, however, did not always come easily, but the Landscape Angel helped, as with the following:

Try less ink. You are not wrong in your dealing with the deva of the machine, but you do not consider it enough. It can help more, and the printing will be more of a two-way affair, as you widen your consciousness and allow God's life into all departments. There will be less strain; necessary adjustments will pop into your mind as you relax. Try this more and you will find you can contact the deva directly instead of through me. At present you trust me, not it.

We began to think of other machines as in some sense living. Although for some time I had been aware that my typewriter felt different if someone else used it, I had not until then tried to treat it as a live entity. My car definitely responded to love and consideration. Later we came across a remarkable man from the south of England who had long worked with these principles and who, among other things, got almost twice as much mileage from his particular car than other people get from the same model, because he cooperated with the car deva. When he needed a parking space, he would ask the angels to go ahead and clear one for him. It worked, for him. Well, we too can try it!

Later, when we had a maintenance crew instead of just Pete, various machine devas united to say:

We wish to emphasise the truth that all machines respond to human love and caring. You all know this is true. You all have had examples of it, but have usually not registered these examples because they seem nonsensical to the mind. We would not belittle the mind, for through it we were brought to birth, but behind it, empowering it, are forces of even greater strength which we would ask you to use when you deal with machines. Metals are part of the one life; treat them as such and you will get a response. Bring joy to the world of metal by cooperating with us also.

This message, I think, was helpful to the building and gardening crews who used metal implements, and for a while at least the tool shed was spick and span with shiny tools. But we had further lessons to learn regarding our awareness of machines and Nature. The owner of the trailer park hired a bulldozer to flatten some ground nearby, and we borrowed it to bulldoze a hill on our land. When I heard about this and saw the results, I felt quite sick at the way the vegetation — mostly gorse and grass — and the land had been torn up and pushed around, and was not surprised to hear that Ogilvie in Edinburgh was told by

106

the nature spirits that all was not well at Findhorn, that we had been maltreating them again. The devas confirmed that the bulldozing brought disharmony and was an example of man following his own pursuits regardless of anything else. They said they had been accustomed to this approach from man, but would be delighted if it would cease, and implied that it was high time we stopped asking questions and got on with real cooperation. However, bulldozing continued on the land we were using, although not by us, and according to Ogilvie the nature spirits living in the ground left the area. The devas did not say 'I told you so'; they suggested that we apply the principles of wholeness to the situation. Had we considered the dwellers in the ground? Had any of us sought to ameliorate in any way the harshness for them of the workings of the machine? Did any of us apologise for the harm done? Man cannot wash his hands of any action done by any one, for we are all part of life and each of us has a responsibility to act from wholeness.

Working with machines as conscious parts of life opens, I believe, an enormous new field for human exploration. Science fiction has caught this vision, albeit in a perverse manner. In this technological age, such a holistic attitude can lead to vast changes in the quality of human and other life on Earth.

Sometimes this attitude is used in technology albeit unconsciously. I have been told that there is a small group of modern geniuses, computer experts, and some of the most highly paid men in the world, who travel the world to mend computers. What they do is sit near the machine in silence for a time, concentrating. When they tune into what is wrong they proceed to fix it. There is more than one way of attunement!

When a smile
touches our hearts,
when the forest
stills us to peace,
when music moves us to rapture,
when we really love,
or laugh or dance with joy,
we are one with the angels.

Chapter 8

Angels and Humans: Contrasts and Contacts

Having presented a few examples of angels of different dimensions, I should like now to explore their characteristics to see whether human relationships with them are relevant at this time, apart from a joint working cooperation in a garden.

In my first breakthrough, my sense of the Pea Deva was that it was speaking from a remote distance, remote in that humans and angels were separated because their ways ·were different and they didn't particularly care to come close to a mankind bent on spoiling a planet — a 'man-infested' planet. These impressions were confirmed in my subsequest contacts, and although our relationship kept changing, their view of humanity did not resemble a history book version. Not that they ever conveyed a spirit of criticism; on the contrary, they made impersonal, factual statements in love and fun. I also believe that my own understanding, my own sense of guilt about human misdeeds, influenced, however slightly, my translation of devic viewpoints. It is always true that the message, even from the highest levels, is coloured by the person who receives it, by that person's beliefs, vocabulary, sub-conscious, etc.

It is through the mental capacity to perceive and grasp contrasts that we humans are able to enlarge our awareness. We would not see light without the darkness, feel pleasure without the sorrow, know good without a knowledge of evil. The devas presented a striking contrast to this, because they seemed to function without such pairs of opposites. Their views, born out of a unity which humans rarely experience, thus contrasted sharply with our normal worldly views.

My own awareness, and this would hold for others too, I would imagine, is strongly conditioned by my concept of myself. Although I had experienced God as my inner being, I was still primarily identifying with a limiting personality. The devas, on the other hand, functioned freely, joyfully, with a sense of divine connectedness which empowered them to act without limitation. In my first contact with them, we met in a realm of limitless power, which negated my excuses for remaining within my bounds; and each time I contacted them I had to rise to my greater Self. This see-saw movement, this going up and falling back again, was part of my life and had been since I began my periods of God-attunement. The devas almost taunted me:

You cannot bring weights into our world, you cannot come to us unless you are free, childlike and light. Compared to the usual human murkiness, ours is indeed a wonderful world. Yet, if you choose, you can live your everyday life in the very same attitude that you bring to us. You know that you have to drop your burdens to contact us and therefore you know that you can do it. We say, why not do it all the time? It seems strange to keep on the old way when freedom is yours any time you choose. You love the feel of our life; why do you not live in it more often?

Unanswerable logic, and I would try. Full of love for everything, out I would go to work in the garden, and would see beauty in the little plants, the soil, the sounds of the birds, the wind and particularly the silence. Then along would come Peter with his radio on full blast drowning out the silence and the sounds I so loved, and down I would plummet, back to disharmony. Life is a long journey!

But the devas never plummeted. Why? They gave one reason:

Our consciousness is higher than that of humans because, although we deal with matter as much as you do, we could not cut ourselves off from the divine source of power. You humans cut yourselves off from the same source by your thoughts. You have greater powers than we have, but also greater limitations. We are not imprisoned by the lower form; you need not be, and you will not be when you identify with that source.

We have greater powers? Their tremendous powers were obvious to me, both in the easy flow of their energy and in their use of it in the magical growth of an acorn into an oak or in the force of an earthquake. The angels, as usual, had their own interpretation of power, like the following which was given to me after I had tasted and tuned into the aromatic plant we call wormwood:

Let the power of our plant tune you into the deva world, for you are amazed that so strong a taste can be contained in such a small bit of leaf. But power is our nature — a little root can crack rocks — and power can be used for many purposes.

You humans also have power. You talk of the power of the pen, and there is the power of love or hate, the power you wield in a bulldozer or in a relationship, power on all levels. Yet power is a word which you shy away from because in human hands it is said to be used for evil, to corrupt. We view it in another light entirely. We consider it the greatest gift of God, because with it we can do more for God than without it. We evolve towards more power, that we may be of greater service, and we suggest that power now be considered by you in that context.

The energies of our world and your world are immense; they crowd around, they cry to be unleashed and put to use. Power is everywhere, but so much of it is beyond you, because you are so beset by the limitations imposed by your selfhood. We wield that energy, that power, in vast sweeps, in concentrated nibblings, in vortices, and we wield it right, left and centre as colour, as sound, as anything you can think of. But we wield it according to pattern and for the whole; we wield it with precision for God and to the best of our ability. It is our joy to perfect that power in service.

Will you not do likewise? Why bring yourselves to nothingness by the flawed use of power? Life to us is an expanding glorious change; often to you it is a dreary grind, a purposeless round — and all because you use your opportunities and your power against the whole. It is a ridiculous notion that you can draw to yourselves just what you want without taking the whole into account, and yet this is what you do, what you are educated to do, what the world atmosphere is geared to do. We would have told you this generations ago if you had given us the opportunity!

Joking apart, we do wish to impress on the human world that there is one way to achieve the beautiful use of power: by putting God first. Then all falls into place, and there is the incredible wonder of power wielded in harmony with the whole, as it is with us, in a flashing interchange of beauty leading to ever greater beauty, worlds without end, and without a false move, a strident noise or anything out of keeping, because it would not occur to us to think of ourselves alone. The world is changing, and we would just add to the change and impress on you the purity, beauty, strength and wonder of power used for God. There are no words to express it; find it all within.

This, and similar contrasts, were incentives to me to ponder on the human situation. I would look around and say, 'All very well, but people don't act like that. They use power to trample on others.' But perhaps not basically so; perhaps, like

114

me, they resonated deep down with the devic approach although, like me, they might at times act unlovingly. Anyway, I had to be true to myself.

The devas commented on purity:

In the flower cannot you see matter brought to perfection? You look at humans and see flaws, you look at us and see purity, with any flaws imposed from outside, like dust on our leaves. You, mankind, have the power to create good and evil; we stay above, the little plants stay below, so to speak, and together we remain forever pure, patterned to perfection. Man is similarly patterned, but his knowing is aligned to imperfection, which he therefore manifests. Recognise the One power in us both.

Continual purity, continual love, continual joy, continual flexibility, continual clarity, continual attention; never succumbing to depression, anger, jealousy, or resentment. Wasn't it all boring? Not to their consciousness. Quite the contrary; they couldn't understand our human waste of energy in unfulfilling directions, our constant seeking after something, only to find that it was something else we wanted. In their joyous flows of energy they were satisfied; we never seemed to be. It was we who were living in a dream world, in unreality, for all form is based on unity and all life is one, while we thought otherwise.

But I was still caught in opposites and saw the devas as high up, or far in, and an almost unbridgeable gap existing between them and their farthest reach, the material world which they built. Not so, they said, there are no gaps in Nature. The gap was my own consciousness of separation, for life is like a rope, or a chain of beings, from the highest to the lowest, and one little flick of that rope runs through to cause movement at both ends. It is man who, with his separate sense of selfhood, remains unconscious of the perfect coordination of life. Tune in and find the whole, stop limiting yourselves to the outer levels.

Did they never rest, nor relax? Man could not go on

115

forever as they did, totally dedicated; we were not superhuman. But we were, they said. If we lived fully and completely in the moment, shortcomings would not occur to us. Besides, the angels added,

What fun life is! To hold each little atom in its pattern is to hold it in joy. We see you humans going greyly about your designs, doing things without zest because 'they have to be done', and we marvel that the sparkling life given you could be so filtered down and disguised. Life is abundant joy; each little bite of a caterpillar into a leaf is done with more zest than we sometimes feel in you humans — and a caterpillar has not much consciousness. We should love to shake this sluggishness out of you to make you see that life is ever brighter, flowing, creative, blooming, waxing and waning, eternally one.

At first the devas made sure I realised that their branch of life was always constructive and dealt with life forces in a positive helpful way, while we humans often thoughtlessly and destructively used their handiwork against the common good. They jokingly suggested that it was really surprising that they had not snuffed us out (my words; they would phrase it more delicately). It was obvious that the devas, in their dance of life, served selflessly, while we humans mainly served ourselves. They did not search for answers to the questions of life because they were conscious participants in life's processes. Whereas men have separated, warring wills, they are completely aligned with the will of God. Nature's patterns, though changing with each season, fulfil themselves; whereas, human patterns often seem frozen by the immobility of our minds and our codes, or fractured by our emotions. We drift; devas, anchored to their central point, know what they are about. Man has measured time and bound himself to it; devas do not function in time as we do — they live in the present. Seeing truth, they do not judge.

Yet, though the angelic attitude and the way they live is faultless compared to ours, in some directions human development is potentially greater than their own. For instance, they said, the very contrasts we experience could bring us a greater gift of wonder, a broader view of the many expressions of divine life. Eventually, through experiencing the polarities, we understand love better; through seeing lack, our hearts develop compassion. In fact, the balancing of the pairs of opposites can bring us to a wisdom unattainable by angelic life. Our outstanding contribution to the planet is our developed capacity to love; we can go deeply into the Heart of Love. Our freedom of choice can lead to a more complete creative power than angels possess.

In spite of all our differences, were the devas models for humans? Obviously they were for me; my whole being responded to their dancing joy and freedom, which I sadly lacked. Could I act in the same spirit? I learned more as our relationship progressed. It didn't take long for them to come closer to my consciousness and to lose their remoteness. Our attentive carrying out of their suggestions in the garden broke barriers, until they were almost queuing to contact such cooperative people. The Landscape Angel became a true friend and, in our two-way conversations, stretched and clarified my mind immeasurably. I had a strange experience with one deva, that of a little daisy-like flower called mesembryanthemum which opened its petals only when the sun was out, for I felt like a sister with it. There was a shared closeness which was new to me, and afterwards I decided it was based upon our joint love of and response to the sun. My reaction to the feel of the angelic world was always positive; I loved their joy and lightness, and each time I contacted them I emerged very happy.

Was my relationship unique, or was it common? Well, we are all unique but, as my consciousness of myself and the devas grew, I realised increasingly how much our two lines of life are linked. In developing my links with the angels, I first had to deal with my own blockages: my acknowledged inadequacies, my fear of writing untruth, my doubts, my tenseness, any current negative mood. My God-identity kept encouraging me, saying that communication with the devic realms would be spontaneous for man on many levels when he was more spiritually attuned and his purpose more forceful and positive. So I kept on, hating Peter's questions in case I framed a wrong answer, but loving the high free lightness of angelic consciousness. After a couple of years Peter had acquired sufficient gardening knowledge and had few questions for me and, in my job of welcoming each new plant to the garden, I could roam in their realms.

It took me quite a few years to conclude that these beings and I were communicating freely because we were sharing the same spheres, that of the human soul, or higher self, and that naturally everyone, in attuning to his or her higher self, was also attuning to the angels. They said that humans can function on all levels of the planet; I understood this from an evolutionary perspective, namely that the life force which developed into human consciousness had gone through the development of, and therefore incorporated and understood, mineral, vegetable and animal consciousness, from the stability of a stone on up. I had not taken our higher consciousness into account; now I was aware that angels shared this level with man.

It took me several more years to experience the fact that angels were 'within', like the kingdom of heaven. This did not mean that they were not independent patterns of energy. It only meant that up until then I paid mere lipservice to the devic concepts of Oneness, and that my mind was still functioning in the normal cultural mode that everything perceived through my five senses was outside myself. A sort of farthest-fields-are-greenest orientation was operative which considered devas more interesting when in far-off high realms, even though another sense knew that somehow Oneness was truth. My transformation in viewpoint did not apply to devas alone. I once heard a bird singing inside myself, for instance, an absurd experience which I had had to accept only because it happened. As the Yarrow Deva said of my new recognition of devic Oneness at the time:

Welcome Oneness; do not strive to keep separate. We are not less real nor lessened in any way. Of course it is strange at first. You are afraid you will miss the delight and joy of

118

us, but that too is within. Look at it this way: how can Oneness exist if you reach out of yourself for it? You are simply putting a limitation on yourself, expecting yourself to be what you already know. Have we not always told you of the great potentials humans have? Accept Oneness and rejoice. Bring Oneness and communion with all things into all of your life. Grow. It is a natural growth at this time.

You think you will miss the sense of massed beauty and joy of our world? Oh, perverse human, that too is within. Feel it, feel it vibrating within, closer than breathing. There is nothing lacking. If God, who is All, is within, can you exclude us? Be sensible.

Actually, at that moment I was so uncomfortable with this change that the Yarrow Deva obligingly floated into the usual mould of my consciousness, saying, *'But remember we are one — and I am glad that Oneness is so rampant.'* How we cling to what we know! I suppose my mind was trying to grapple with the fact that every point in the cosmos can be considered its centre. Consciousness is a weird and wonderful thing, and I had, and have, many more revelations in store.

As far as the devic realm was concerned, I was not unique; others were having similar experiences. When we published the original *Findhorn Garden* story and sent it out through our mailing list, we received many letters from all over the world from readers reporting their own devic insights and adventures. Almost all of them wrote that they had not dared to mention such episodes before, for fear of being thought crazy, and added that it was a tremendous relief to read of equivalent happenings.

I became increasingly aware of countless points of contact that we enjoy with this other order of life. For instance, the devas know our minds, our motives, our feelings — and they always have. Like all life, the angels respond to love, and when a human loves some piece of 'matter', the devic counterparts love back in their own way. I have no doubt that this is the secret, or the process, behind people with green thumbs. In all of life, human love and dedication bring their own rewards, often through angelic agencies. Surely the Angels of Sound, or the Muses, cooperated with an almost deaf Beethoven.

Early on they said that we — in this case, those of us who love Nature — often enter into and walk in their world without an awareness of them. They know when we enter, and we know from an added feeling of uplift and freedom. The devas said that when we think about plants, or say, even eating a vegetable, or being under a tree, a closeness is brought about. They also said:

Humans often touch into our worlds, mostly unconsciously, and we are always delighted because here you are free and closer to your real selves. Our land is open to the whole human race, but in order to enter or to stay for more than a fleeting visit, you voluntarily have to give up certain attachments. These wonderful worlds of ours are right here in your midst and always have been, unnoticed because you don't look for them. Infusions from our world seep into man's highest endeavours, into his moments of inspiration and adoration, into his moments of wonder and enchantment, and remain untouched by the scoffing mind.

The devas said that it is man's role to approach them, to effect the communication.

I could accept these ideas, and then I would have moments of doubt and would question the need for devic contact; to my mind the contact with God within was more important and gave a much fuller picture. From within came the answer:

Unity of my ways on all levels is the ideal. All are part of me. I have hands and feet to form my patterns and work my wonders. The devic world is a particularly clear channel, unceasingly living in my ways in purity and beauty, and with marvellous results. Flowers, for example, speak a universal language. The devic world would not divert anyone from my ways, because my ways are all that concern them, and they acknowledge me freely. Their world spans a vast range, from the highest beings to the lowest cell, and this vast chain is firm in its adherence to

120

my ways.

I replied by asking about angelic reaction to man's destructive interference, and was told:

Still they stay within the law. If human treatment causes them and their friends to rebel [I had been thinking of the elves leaving the garden], *then human treatment can cause them to drop their rebellion. When you permeate life with love, you are one with each other and there is no question of division.*

So back I would go to attuning to the devas, and they would reinforce the joy of that contact by sharing more of their world, even commenting that they wanted to work with humans.

Although, of course, our divinity and our angelic selves are innate in all that we do, on occasion they emerge into our experience with stunning clarity. When a beautiful sunset makes us catch our breaths, when the form or scent or colour of a flower humbles us, when we are so enthralled in some action that we lose all sense of time and place, when a smile touches our hearts, when the forests still us to peace, when music moves us to rapture, when we really love, or laugh or dance with joy, we are one with the angels. Meditation techniques can help us to the same sense of oneness, but so can the wonderful world around us. It doesn't matter if, for some, communication with the angels is not as conscious as mine. What really matters is that we have been elevated to a greater sense of being. And an enlarged consciousness deepens our experience.

The devas say that the barriers between our two worlds are breaking down, that:

The initiative for this communion has to come from humans; we are always here. Those of you who do reach to us feel the touch of beauty, of truth, of wonder, and even a sense of homecoming. From this you will know that you have entered our reality and you will wish to come again. You will experience an expansion of spirit, and you will

*be refreshed. We too are refreshed, because for too long
there has been separation between our realms to the detri-
ment of both.*

*We cannot come to you, but we notice, appreciate and
respond when you come to us. Your thrust of appreciation
of beauty, of truth and reverence, for a brief moment
makes us one. Generally this does not last; you have not
the courage of your convictions, nor the practice to remain
with us. We say, relax, shed your old knowledge, be as
children, and simply come. It does not matter if we do not
interchange in language or thought. We know that if
humanity could feel our realms, life on Earth would be
completely changed. It would be the best move ever made
by man, for we would not keep you but would pass you
on in consciousness to the One of whom we are ever conscious, the Life and Light of the World, which we rejoice
in forever.*

*This is related to your garden and to your life. This is
growth.*

I could understand the meaning of the angels' passing us
on in consciousness to God. Their awareness was so expansive,
so loving and so full of thanksgiving that I could not help but be
aware of a greater Presence. It was a lovely feeling, but it was
always challenging for me to remain in an expanded awareness,
especially when other people were around. Hermits, I thought,
with no one to gainsay them, had an easy life of it; why was I in
a group of people? Devas were much easier to communicate
with than humans, because devas went beyond the surface
straight to the reality of a person. Perhaps the devas had that
fact in mind when they said that man would be astonished at
the ease with which communication with the angels would
come. I was inclined to dismiss that statement as fantasy; the
devas said no, I was at last touching reality. It was our human
difficulties, our problems, our evils which were fantasies. The
worlds that angels and humans shared were the reality, and they
would seek to make this clear to us.

I thought all this was wonderful, but what of the realities

I had to live with? What about the increasing rape of Nature, the disappearance of the wilderness areas? What about man's destruction of the world through the pollution of the land, the waters, and the air? I was told that these were the consequences of man's lack of contact with devas, that when we turn to devic reality and become aware of the truth of their existence, we will no longer break the laws of our joint worlds. We will all know that although we may be two distinct orders of life, we cannot be separated and we cannot live to ourselves alone. The devas said:

> *This fact is becoming plain to the ordinary man all over the world, but the living vitality behind this fact you experience as you turn to us and feel the love and oneness which we are. On our level we extend our love to mankind, for such is the will of God and we have no life outside that will. Your welcome is ensured; will you come quickly?*

I have been approached by people eager to see devas — by which they almost always mean fairies — and they think that I can tell them how to go about it. They have either tried without results, or they would love to try. What is my technique? Their awe of me rapidly expires when I flatly reply that I have never seen them either, or that astral vision is a retrograde step for mankind, or that I don't believe it matters. Also, because everyone is different and each has his own unique contribution to make to life, no two contacts with the angelic world would be quite the same. Yet I can understand the glamour of it. Fairy lore abounds with legends of enchantment, of wishes coming true, of people who were never the same after a visit to fairyland. There is deep truth behind these tales, the same truth contained in the phrase that a moment with the Lord is better than an eternity without him.

However, for any nature lovers who feel specifically drawn to conscious communion with the devas of the plant world, here are some angles that I found helpful. Again, this communion starts from the highest level of our being, and the more divine we know it to be, the better. If I am free from worry, it is easiest for me to feel harmonious when I am outdoors, where I quickly reach a state of diffused delight and happiness. This state needs to be focused on the essence of the particular plant. The season of flowering, of the fullest expression of the plant, gives the most clues to its essence through its colour, shape and scent, and the uniqueness of leaf and stem. In winter the energy is withdrawn. If I couldn't get the feel of its essence, I would live with the plant for a while, even picking a flower to keep in my room. Any particular meaning that the plant had for me, or any personal knowledge of it, created a link. Straining for contact only built barriers, whereas Love and appreciation build togetherness. I believe that there may be some plants with which one cannot easily harmonise. I couldn't attune to the Wallflower, so just respected it and moved on — and now wonder whether my block came from the unpleasant teenage memories that its name evoked!

The angels suggested that we tune into Nature until there was a love flow, saying the the natural world responds to our state of being, to what we are, not to what we say or do. If we are depressed or if our minds are going around in circles, we will not find harmony with the devas; however, by being open to the influence of Nature, we will lose the depression and find peace. Then the love flow can start and the attunement can follow. They suggest that we bring our problems to them, explaining that a recognition of and appeal to them is always answered in some way. But first, in order to have our minds open enough to receive their more complete knowledge, we must discard our human preconceptions. There is no need to consider *how* the angels will drop an idea into our minds. Once that idea has been registered, we can again make use of our intellects for the best means of carrying out their suggestion. The devas say that they are the source of our inspiration in many fields, including science. After all, they wield the laws of the universe all the time, and when man is ready they will share their knowledge.

But the angels have more to offer us than relieving our depressions or answering our questions. To me, their whole living style, their approach to reality, is relevant to our human condition and can help us. But before I go more deeply into their perceptions, I will share a theme the tree devas want to impart to mankind.

Great forests must flourish,
and man must see to this
if he wishes to continue to live on this planet.
We are, indeed, the skin of the Earth,
and a skin not only covers and protects,
but passes through it
the forces of life.

Leylands Cypress Deva

Chapter 9

The Message of the Large Trees

I have always loved trees. There is something deeply appealing about them, something peaceful yet grand, and to me a walk through the woods is a cure for my upsets. For me, trees, and particularly large trees, have a splendour unmatched by other plants, raising my aspiration, ennobling one part of me, steadying another part, enriching my spirit. Living in an area bereft of trees brings me a sense of privation, and Findhorn, like other wind-swept peninsulas and most of the Hebridean Isles, was bare. Scots Pine was the only species acknowledged to be viable there, and fortunately a neighbour had already planted a small shelter belt of these, which also prevented some of our sandy soil and plants from being blown away.

Though the trailer park was treeless, except for a tiny apple orchard that we had planted, before the year was out my love of trees had led to a contact with the Scots Pine Deva. There was a strong and solid feel that distinguished this deva from those of other plants. Confirming my feeling that trees had healing power and much to give to humans, the angel added:

We are guardians of the Earth in many ways, and humans should be a part of what we guard. We are not active young things; we are, in a way, like a school of benevolent philosophers with unhuman purity and a great wish to serve humanity. Trees are vital to man and to life on this planet, and some of us are eager to experience this contact with some humans before others destroy what we have built up.

It was lovely to contact a tree deva, but I forgot about them until the Landscape Angel brought to my awareness a group of large tree devas. They explained that, naturally, they had to be brought to me, as there were no large trees around. This could not be helped, they said, but:

We would emphasise the absolute necessity for large trees for the well-being of the land. This is not merely because we [the tree devas] partly control rainfall, but we also draw forth inner radiances which are as necessary to the land as rain. Because we know of the importance of your experiment and of our contribution to it, we are lending our forces here. Even without trees, this will have a certain effect, and we can also be drawn by love from any of you. So let us come into your hearts now and again, and perhaps sometime we will find our way into the ground.

To Peter's obedient and willing mind this was tantamount to a command. He decided to cultivate trees. We bought a hundred two-year-old seedlings, and we scoured the countryside for more. The Forestry Commission planted such trees by driving a spade into the ground twice, making a cross shape, and placing the seedling in the central space. Wherever he found space, Peter planted baby trees in this easy manner. The large tree devas were delighted with our action, and said that they would speed up growth because they needed fully grown trees for a real influence — like humans, whose children cannot do the job as an adult. For about a year, until they were established, my favourite occupation became the evening watering of these small conifers. In the process, which included my thinking 'big' for the trees, I became convinced that there is some more potent cooperative way of accelerating tree growth. I am still convinced, if still ignorant of it.

Several years went by. For part of that time I had a local secretarial job which took me away from contacting angels. People began to join our group and to settle in sites adjoining ours. To act as a windbreak for flowers that he proposed to grow by a new trailer, Peter put in a fastgrowing cypress hedge. Early in 1967, in my job of welcoming all new plants into the garden, I attuned to the deva of this species, the Monterey Cypress, and the most vehement blast of consciousness that I had yet encountered came at me. I translated it as follows:

We come in with a lordly sweep, for we are not just the small trees that you see in your garden, but denizens of the magnificent spaces of great hills in the sun and wind. We put up with being hedges, but always in our inner being is this growing toward the open sun-kissed places where we stand in clustered grandeur.

You feel in us an almost intolerable longing to be fully ourselves. We of the plant world have our pattern and destiny, worked out through the ages, and we feel it quite wrong that, because of man and his encroachment, we and others like us are not allowed to be. We have our portions of the plan to fulfil; we have been nurtured for this very reason, and now, in this age, many of us can only dream of the spaces where we can fulfil ourselves. The pattern is ever before us, out of reach, a chimera we are forever growing toward but seldom attaining. The planet needs the likes of us in our full maturity. We are not a mistake on the part of Nature; we have work to do.

Man is now becoming controller of the world forests and is beginning to realise how much these are needed. But he covers acres with one quickgrowing species, selecting trees for silly economic reasons with no awareness at all of the planet's needs. This shows utter ignorance of the purpose of trees and their channelling of diverse forces. The world needs us on a large scale. Perhaps if man were in tune with the infinite, as we are, and were contributing his share, the forces would be in balance. But at present the

planet needs more than ever just what is being denied it:
the forces which come through the large and stately trees.

I was agitated by the sense of urgency coming to me, and the deva as good as apologised for the broadsides aimed at me as a human listener. On registering that I felt entirely inadequate to do anything about these facts, the angel comforted me by saying that I was looking at the situation from a limited level, that communicating with humans helped, because a truth once in human consciousness then percolates around and does its work. And they felt better for communicating! However, when I passed this message to Peter and Eileen, I think they mistook my intensity for a personal attack on them for the very ordinary act of planting a hedge, despite my protests to the contrary, and they seemed completely unresponsive to the message. In any case, their concern was for Findhorn. Of course, their attitude made me feel even more frustrated.

It took me some years to perceive the truth in the devic statement about thoughts filtering through human consciousness. How often is some invention developed at the same time in different places — in America Edison is credited with the invention of the electric light bulb; in Britain Swann is. Now, in ecology movements all over the world there is great awareness of many of the points that the tree devas made, although many more open minds are needed. Nevertheless, among the numerous members of the angelic world that I contacted, the large tree devas were the only ones with a strong sense of urgency, of importance, of relevance. They were trying to tell us something, and so I will continue with their message.

The Scots Pine Deva, speaking for the large trees in general, next took up the theme:

We thank humanity for planting us so extensively and enabling us to reclaim much territory. You see, trees act as a protective skin to the Earth and in that skin bring about necessary changes. We devas are outer sentinels of that change, able to do our work where others could not. We glory in this; our high praise goes forth like scent from a flower. It blesses all who come and rest in our aura, in our forests, although self-absorbed humans are unconscious of our influence. Trees, rooted guardians of the surface, converters of the higher forces to Earth through the ground, have a special gift for man in this age of speed and drive and busy-ness. We are calmness, strength, endurance, praise, and fine attunement, all of which are greatly needed in the world. We are more than that. We are expressions of the love of the Creator for his abundant, unique and related life. We have purpose. We could not do without one another, however isolated or self-sufficient we may be geographically. The whole of life is here now, and it is our privilege to sound our special note. Come to our side whenever you can, and lift your consciousness.

While other trees came to my awareness and talked of various aspects of Nature, another cypress was the one to suggest that men and trees be more creative, mindful of the need to serve on the widest scale.

Let us not be niggardly in the future. Vast areas need us, and by us I mean large trees in general. We simply cannot emphasise this enough. We are the skin of this world; take us away and the complete planet, no longer able to function, dries up and dies. Let us be, and the whole creature purrs with contentment, and life goes on in natural sequence, becoming ever more aware of unity.

It is a fact that if a certain percentage of the skin on any creature is destroyed that creature perishes. I wondered if the deva had any glimpse of that for the world, or any idea of the future. Obviously the deva did not think in such linear terms, for it replied:

If the future is better than the past, we glimpse it. Man has made us more conscious of our functions by his interference, and thus good has inadvertently come. Together, a better world can result.

133

Other tree devas also felt a concern for the planet. The Rowan (Mountain Ash) Deva talked of the diminishing portion of the Earth being left in its natural state, and made a plea for us to be guided in our control of the land by following Nature's ways. We must always remember that each plant has a place in the whole. Other tree devas said trees help man keep mental stability, and there could be large woodlands near big cities for this purpose. Another Cypress Deva, with its strong 'voice', again mentioned the need for the surface of the earth to have large trees, continuing:

The planet cries out for us in bulk, but man, intent on his own devices, goes his way oblivious. We remain overlighting, ready to play our part as always. We have been so much part of the destiny of this world, so indispensable to man, that we cannot envisage a world without the return of the forests.

I asked whether the vibrational level of the whole planet would be so different in the new age that the physical world would change greatly and trees would not be needed as much? No, said the deva:

There have been mighty changes in the past as this Earth has evolved but, while the sun shines and life depends on water, our role has been necessary and will continue to be. All of life will change, will be lighter and happier and more aware, but nevertheless we have much to do. Our purposes flow as strongly as ever. We feel them coursing through us in waves of strength from the Source, and we seize every opportunity to tell man of the need for the forests. We would reach his mind that he may know, without a doubt, of this necessity. Man has taken on only part of his role as a creative Son of God and is acting without the wisdom needed to fulfil that role. We attempt to make this clear to him. What is important now is consciousness. Our nature worlds are essential; much of man's worlds, created with a sense of separation, is not essential. Together we can create a better earth.

I felt in harmony with all these points about the use of trees and, one day, full of gratitude for the serenity found with the trees, asked if there was anything I could do for them. The Tree Devas answered:

You can render the greatest of services by recognising us and bringing our reality to human consciousness. It is fact that we are many, yet speak with one clear voice; it is fact that we are the overlighting intelligence of each species, not the spirits of individual trees; it is fact that we are vitally concerned with the Earth as a whole. Because we see mankind interfering detrimentally with the unit which you call this planet, we would communicate with him to make him more aware of divine law. The devas have been part of human growth in the distant past; we are part of that growth now, growth which has led him to self-consciousness and now to god-consciousness. Recognise our role, recognise God's life in all. Mankind as a whole does not recognise us. You can strongly emphasise that Nature is not a blind force, that it is conscious and has inner vehicles. Then man, as he comes to truth, will recognise us with his higher mind in spite of his intellect, and then he will fulfil God's purposes. We are grateful for any spreading of this truth.

So would I have been, but I was a voice crying in the wilderness — and not being a pushy person, an extremely feeble voice. I kept on getting more messages, for instance, when I visited a wonderful tree garden on the west coast near Ullapool, which contained many specimens of large trees including redwoods. There I felt more clearly the function of large trees as conductors of energy, standing ever ready and channelling universal forces of especially potent vibrations. There were magnificent groups of sentinels in that garden, seemingly rooted and upraised to cosmic energies, vibrant in peace and transforming power. The devas repeated that large trees were essential for planetary welfare, saying that their disappearance was but another sign of the troubled times at the end of an age.

I was becoming somewhat paranoid about my inability to spread the message of the large trees, when Richard St. Barbe Baker visited Findhorn. St. Barbe is the founder of the Society of the Men of the Trees, initiator of the Forestry Commission in Britain and writer of many books on trees, including **Sahara Conquest**. His untiring and life-long work with trees throughout the world (he was over 80) had brought him to the same views as expressed by the angelic world, although his approach had been scientific and practical. This confirmation was a tremendous joy and tonic to me. I felt a closeness to this man, and when Peter and I toured the site for St. Barbe to treescape the area, I found that I knew what he was going to say, that we had the same views, although I did not know the names of plants and shrubs. It was perhaps not surprising, therefore, that the only message concerning a person that I have so far received from the angelic world came from the Deva of Leylands Cypress about St. Barbe, after he had ceremonially planted some of these fastgrowing trees in the caravan park:

There is high rejoicing in our kingdoms as the Man of the Trees, so beloved of us, links with you here. Is it not an example in your worlds that it is one world, one work, one cause under God being expressed through different channels? Rejoice and let the plan unfold. I am, of course, speaking on behalf of all the Tree Devas, who have naturally long been overlighting the Man of the Trees, and we wish to express our deepest thanks to him. We hope he has always known of our gratitude for what he has done, and we would like to emphasise it in this way.

You understand better now why we have gone on and on and on about the need for trees on the surface of the Earth. Great forests must flourish, and man must see to this if he wishes to continue to live on this planet. The knowledge of this necessity must become part of his consciousness, as much accepted as his need for water in order to live. He needs trees just as much; the two are

interlinked. We are, indeed, the skin of the Earth and a
skin not only covers and protects, but passes through it
the forces of life. Nothing could be more vital to life as a
whole than trees, trees and more trees.

St. Barbe's visit sparked a greater interest in trees, which culminated in 1970 in the group publishing Part Four of the original *Findhorn Garden* story. This section, called 'Talking Trees', consisted of unedited messages receiving from various tree devas. St. Barbe wrote a foreword to this which included:

> The messages from Tree Devas through Dorothy reveal the occult explanation that scientific research has been unable to give. The ancients believed that the Earth itself is a sentient being and feels the behaviour of mankind upon it. As we have no scientific proof to the contrary, I submit that we accept this and behave accordingly, and thus open up for ourselves a new world of understanding. How dull life would be if we did not accept anything we could not explain! For my part, I would rather be a believer than an unbeliever. It would be conceited to be otherwise, when there is the miracle of sunrise and sunset in the Sahara, the miracle of growth from the tiny germinating seed to the forest giant — a veritable citadel, in itself providing food and shelter for myriads of tiny things and an indispensable link in the Nature cycle, giving the breath of life to man.

Before the publication of our little booklet on trees, I had run away for a weekend to be alone with the large trees left in a remnant of the ancient Caledonian Forest in the Beinn Eighe Nature Reserve. It was a strange, distressing experience, because although protected, the few trees left (the area had been logged, of course) seemed to be dying out without regenerating themselves. The Pine Deva said that age and a changing world had caused crystallisation, that the trees needed a rarified air of solitude or to be with harmonious people, that the 'feyness' of the Scot was related and was dying with the old pines. I asked if the

trees could return and was told that they could, in a more understanding and loving world, a world that would call on them in
sufficient strength and provide the right conditions. This was in
the hands of man. Feeling very sad, and not simply because of
the constant rain, I asked if the trees were sad. Yes, I was told,
sad that trees and the stalwart and enduring qualities that they
brought to Earth were not appreciated, sad that this would result
in lack of endurance, lack of independence and lack of love of
Nature among men. Again I was told that trees were an integral
part of the whole, to be respected, loved, cherished and thanked
by man.

That man receives more than wood from trees was again
brought to my attention by another large tree deva, this time
not a conifer but a copper beech. I had been attuning to the
many small flowers planted around new caravans and had been
receiving a series of delightfully joyous but rather high, trilling
messages, and the firm, strong vibrations of the trees were certainly a relief. The Copper Beech Deva said that I needed to feel
the steady flow of its force, that all people gained by partaking
of this balancing energy, this firm foundation, especially in the
world of lost values which man was inhabiting at present. I had
touched on yet another reason for large trees:

*We channel a type of force that has a steadying influence
on life. Truth tells you to build your foundations on rock,
on God, which is what we do and what we unconsciously
remind you to do. Man does not realise that, among other
things, his natural environment is full of forces that corres-
pond to, and therefore can bring out, some part of his own
makeup, and that he is influenced by his environment in
many subtle ways. Here, too, the great trees have a mighty
part to play, and you are bereft of some part of yourself
and of your heritage when you denude the land of large
trees.*

Here again was a forceful message, and I was glad that it
had come in time to be included in the little booklet sent out to
our mailing list. The limited audience that the booklet reached

138

was at least a beginning. Nevertheless, the tree devas did not let up on their theme. While visiting an Adult Education College in England that generated a lot of mental energy, the Cedar of Lebanon Deva spoke to me of counterbalancing bright ideas with inner peace, as the enormous limbs of the cedars were balanced in peace and so were able to withstand storms. The deva mentioned the divine power that trees stabilise, and the kinship of life, saying:

> *You and I are blood brothers, made from the same substance, each fulfilling his destiny on this planet. I contain you in my towering strength; you contain me in your towering aspiration. We are much more than tree and human. We are representatives of divinity, going on from strength to strength through the endless ages. You can enrich the Earth with your enlightened love, which we cannot do through our Earth patterns, but we too can be a channel for new energies in our openness and acceptance of them, without the block of thought.*

Certainly the magnificent cedar trees there gave an impression of endless strength, as did the great oaks. The Oak Deva, after we had greeted the sunrise together and it had reiterated the planetary need of trees, talked of there being a great love between man and oak, built up through their long connections. This thought reminded me of an incident in my caravan, which was almost completely lined in light oak. I had been admiring the grain of the wood one day, when I wondered if there were still any devic connections with these pieces of 'dead' matter. Yes, I gathered, and human appreciation at once creates a link with the devic world and adds to the fullness of life.

When the time came for me to leave Findhorn, I was lucky enough to go almost immediately to an area full of large trees, over 5,000 feet up, on the slopes of Mt. Lassen in California. I was awed and enthralled by the wonderful stands of Ponderosa pine, incense cedar, sugar pine and trembling aspen, all being lovingly protected on a private ranch. I thankfully walked under these huge, if still immature, trees — the area had been logged several times, though not within the last fifty years. But I did not attempt to contact the devic forces; I couldn't. I was too painfully torn. From dawn to dusk great logging trucks thundered by every five minutes (I timed them), transporting large tree trunks to the mills, charging dangerously along because the drivers were paid on a time basis. Empty trucks, driven even more dangerously, headed back for refills at the lumber stands. Transporting trees to mills in the opposite direction, but on a dirt road through the forests and therefore at a slower pace, were the similarly loaded trucks of a different company, and their empty returning vehicles. Near by, Forestry Service trees were being felled. There was nowhere to go to get away from the sound of logging operations — and I have since had the same experience elsewhere in the Sierras.

When I could sufficiently pull myself together to approach the tree devas and apologise for our human behaviour, they greeted me as follows:

Child of Earth and spirit, we address the spirit aspect of your nature, for that is our meeting ground. As you have felt, we are not in harmony with the part of mankind which rapes the land, and nowhere is the cleft between us more recently pronounced than in areas of ancient trees now being thoughtlessly felled.

The devas repeated that, with a dearth of mature trees, the peace and stability of mankind is affected — that we destroy ourselves when we destroy the trees. In spite of the continuing logging sounds, it was a wonderful place to be, immersed in the high vibrating yet grounded tree energies that passed on stability, strength and everlastingness, amid waterfalls, rocks, canyons, hot and cold springs, wild animals and other wilderness marvels.

About a year later I finally had an opportunity to talk on the theme of large trees, now so much a part of me, to an appropriate audience, members of the U. S. Forestry Service.

Miraculously, a workshop with the Forestry Service had been arranged and I found myself on a tiny plane emerging through snow-peaked mountains, as a mote in the azure spaciousness. Down below, the shadow of the plane made a slight ripple

140

over the rugged country that spread out in glorious panorama. At the moment, however, our attention was less on the scenery than on the immediate necessity of finding a landing spot in the midst of all this wilderness. Even the wonder and strangeness of finding myself in this situation, a participant in a special expedition deep into the little-explored fastness of the area, was replaced by the mundane chore of comparing a Forestry Service map with the terrain that spread beneath my window, trying to determine just where we were.

We were flying to a ranger station in a National Forest, but only one of our party had ever been there before and that had been by road. Near it, we knew, was a small landing strip, but we could only see a road slicing the high plateau. We had to be very sure that we landed in the right place. Our plane did not have sufficient power to take off again in that altitude with its four passengers, and once down at the wrong place, we would be stranded and faced with a long trek back to civilisation or, more probably, we would need to be rescued. Above all, we would be unable to keep our rendezvous with the forest rangers.

This journey was important to me. Not only was it an opportunity to attune with Nature and gratify my deep love for wilderness areas; more significantly, it was an unexpected invitation to share my work and experience with people who could most understand and benefit from it, but who, or so I imagined, might be least open to it.

Our plane began to descend. Our pilot had spotted a wide area on the road which seemed to be the landing strip we were looking for. If it was the right one, we would be met by rangers, who would then take us to the station where we would assemble. Our group would then drive many rough miles by bus before backpacking to a remote canyon, which was our final destination and the site of our workshop. On the return trip we would drive almost a hundred miles from the station to an airport on the edge of a cliff, from which our small plane could become airborne.

We flew over some buildings without arousing any response and landed in a flurry of dust. We climbed out into a stark, dry landscape, with nothing in sight, not even a tree. When no one arrived, our hearts began to sink. Had we chosen the wrong site after all? Then, to our relief, a jeep appeared and we were soon on our way. The U.S. Forestry Service and the pagan gods of Nature were about to converge! I hoped both would benefit.

After a long and breathtaking journey, we eventually reached our campsite. There, after an excellent and much appreciated meal cooked by the rangers, we sat around the campfire in the dark, like tribesmen after a hunt, while I, in the ancient tradition of the shaman, told my stories of the overlords and intelligences behind Nature and of my experiences with them. Were it not for our cultural conditioning, we might have been a group from five thousand years ago. We weren't, however. We were men and women of the twentieth century, trained to look for scientific proof before we could believe, trained to think in terms of distinct empirical facts and to demand such facts as the admission price of our acceptance of an idea. At least, that is how we like to think of ourselves, however seldom we truly live up to that ideal, for our culture has its own superstitions. One of them is that the institution of science is the best, if not the only, path to truth. In the dark I couldn't see the men's expressions, and after I had finished there was dead silence. In silence we all dispersed to our tents or sleeping bags — a tent for me, regretfully, since I love sleeping under the stars, but we had spotted several rattlers earlier, and I was told that they often crawled into sleeping bags for warmth. I fell asleep still wondering whether the men had accepted or rejected my views.

The next day we interacted with exercises and attunements. By the end of the workshop on the third day most of the men had individually told me that the devic messages had revived in them their own deep feelings for Nature which had been pushed down since childhood. These men, when asked why they had joined the Forestry Service in the first place, generally made replies like 'I wanted to get away from people.' Now they were admitting their love for and kinship with Nature, for it had been that which had called them into their profession. Each of them was a Nature mystic in his own way, however unrecognised that might be. Therefore, I felt we were able to communicate. I certainly was well received, and when we parted after our return to civilisation, plans were made for me to give more seminars on talking to the angels. As all I would ever want a workshop to do is help to relate people to their own inner realities, I was content with this one.

But obviously, much more than a few workshops are required to safeguard even our remaining trees. I have seen giant redwoods with plaques on them stating that they are part of the primeval forest to be preserved forever for posterity, as this stand had been gifted for this pupose by so and so. And I look at the tip of these great trees and see that already they are dying — dying because man has created dams that keep back the yearly floods that nourish them, dying because of automobile pollution, or dying because the earth around them has been compacted by human feet.

Obviously, many factors have to be considered. Are we in fact despoiling the surface of the planet in our forest felling? Do we have to use so much wood for building and for newsprint? Should we or should we not fight all forest fires? With greater ecological awareness and with greater ingenuity, we can find solutions. Increasingly the angelic assertions are being proved correct, and certainly we can only find lasting solutions when we consider the whole of the planet, when we view it in the way the angels view it. I believe we are perfectly capable of doing this.

You humans
cling to the known.
You even expect
one another to always be the same,
instead of realising that you are creatures
different from what you were
in the last second of time,
and that you have
infinite possibilities
to be still more
different.

The Devas

Chapter 10

Creative Living Styles

Although the messages from the tree devas were the most urgent ones imparted to me, there were other themes both implicit and explicit in the devic communications. The angels wanted to share with humans and to help us realise the integrated, abundant life that we could lead together. From the very first message, they referred to the fact that human potential was tremendous but, like an iceberg, only a small segment was showing. They had to keep repeating this to me because I was so split, seeing and identifying with, yet wanting to deny, the 'bad' personality part of myself, and yet very aware, through both training and experience, of the 'good' part. The devas attempted to make me whole. For me, the mechanics of contact with them was an education in itself, as each time I had to identify with my higher self.

Once I was in that higher or devic part of myself, the devas could naturally communicate straight to me. They were true educators in the etymological sense of bringing out of, drawing out of me qualities rarely expressed. They were joyful, so I would resonate to their joy and soon I would be joyful. Then they could talk about joy, or whatever it was that they wanted to share at the time. In fact they said:

*We devas would like to dance around in the consciousness
of every human being to wake you up to what you are. We
would have you know that you are light beings and not
confined to your physical presence. Simply because you
think that you are so confined, you remain so, but when
you are aware of us and come to our level, you are part of
a larger world which is also home to you. You have
awakened to what you have always been, and it is sometimes easier to recognise this when it is formulated for
you. So we formulate now the lightness, joy, speed and
intelligence which you are and which we are, and there is
much more we have left unsaid as yet. So join us often to
be educated about yourself, and do it in the love of
the One.*

That was lovely. My consciousness would be dancing for a
while, and maybe after each visit the dance lasted a little longer.
My consciousness and the consciousness of humanity was
important to them. In 1968, particularly, their messages definitely shifted to the realm of human consciousness, speaking of
new vibrations for man to incorporate.

Before consciousness can be expanded, it is well to be
aware of our subconscious natures and of the ruts we follow.
Take prejudice, for example. I thought that I was fairly free
of prejudice, having lived in several cultures, in several different
racial psyches, but the angels thought otherwise:

*Among humans it rarely happens that you all unite in re-
ceiving and passing on the current expressions of life, because generally you are not open. You have your own
separative thoughts, your own little worlds which you
carry with you, your own opinions which exclude the
opinions of others. You cut yourself off from truth by
having 'axes to grind' and personal interests. Because of
our universal interest, we are open to anything and so receive various waves of communication without hindrance.
How difficult this is for you! You are each conditioned
by your background and enclosed in its memory, while*

we are free to be unique yet open to another's contribu-
tion. You emphasise and are guided by your environmen-
tal differences; we thank God that we are individually
different and therefore together make the One. Try to
listen to life without prejudice. You are more than that
small pattern of behaviour created by your past. You are
free, clear, expressive sons of God, all of you. Drop the
limitations of prejudice. Be alert to life, and then its
communications can run through you like a ripple of
laughter, or a deep deep understanding. All is of the
One when you allow it to be.

On another occasion the devas seemed almost harassed by
the way the beauty of the plant world was expressed and the
way the beauty of humanity was not expressed, asking:

Why do you not let life grow in you as we do? Why do
you put brakes on, or divert your energy into habits which
you have long outgrown? You have your codes, your sys-
tems, your ways of life which you may have found useful
in the past, but which to us only seem to check the God-
energy within you. We have our patterns, but the life
force flows easily and perfectly into them, and fulfils
them. You have your patterns, but the energy seems to
flow anywhere but into its true ones. We see you imita-
ting one another, following current fashions, doing some-
thing because you always have, choosing from habit, or,
in other words, closing yourselves off from the life urge
within you. What a waste, when you have this most won-
derful God-energy within which, if followed, would make
a paradise on this Earth! Why go around like zombies,
following this or that external guide when all the time
your only guide is within you?

They wanted to push me out of my mental cages and get
me flowing with change. Their advice was always a continua-
tion of what life and my inner guidance was teaching me;
lessons seem to come from all sides when there is need to learn.

149

I had already been given many opportunities to be willing to change and move by my husband's love of secrecy. I remember John arriving home one day in the 1940's, brandishing two airplane tickets for us to leave in about an hour's time for some faraway country. When I irascibly asked about a dinner date we had that night, he said that it didn't matter and that our friends would not mind if we cancelled it. My subsequent departure was unwilling, as my inclinations to vegetate as well as to keep my word were very strong. I was still learning flexibility, and the devas confirmed that life was mutable, that to cope with the angelic world we had to be willing to accept constant change. As they said:

> There is nothing static in the worlds of the One who forever expresses life and love in an outgoing manner. How then can anything stay as it was? Yet we notice again and again that you humans cling to the known, that you dislike change, that you are disappointed when you find it, that you even expect one another to be always the same, instead of realising that you are creatures different from what you were in the last second of time, and that you have infinite possibilities to be still more different.
>
> Nothing is what it was. Even man's creations become outdated or deteriorate. We who live in and wield to perfection a world of moving energy, would have man join us in the creation of this perfection. Then even the perfection will change. Among men there is far too much preservation of things and ideas. You should step into our worlds to experience more directly the scintillating whirls of life forever on the move. Then you will realise that to keep up with life, to be part of the Oneness of all, there is nothing to cling to but the One who, forever the same, forever changes. Life is always fluctuating. If you get stuck in some rut, we will try to dislodge you. Think of us and our vital changing worlds, and rise to be expressive of life again.

The devic qualities of change, of flexibility, were one of

the most helpful aspects of my contact. The angels were delightful in the way that they would lead me out of limitation, frisking quickly from one thing to another. Or they would comment strongly on some subject, then remind me that what they had said was but one small aspect of the whole. Or I would get used to the feel of a certain deva, then that being would present an entirely different face, to remind me that the whole has many parts, but only one facet is presented at a time. The quicksilver devic qualities were great fun, giving me valuable training not to judge by the past or by appearances. The devic presentation of change is confirmed by science, which has found that Nature is not composed of building blocks, but is a complicated web of relationships. Subatomic particles are not things, but interactions; the universe is an endless display of energy and motion.

The quality of joy was perhaps the most outstanding characteristic of the devic world. Joy was something I resonated with deeply. I always have, although I experienced little joy until my periods of attunement with God. Yet on the surface I was not joyful, much as I wished that I were. There is a link between our weak and our strong points; we are like Demosthenes, who, because of a stammer, practised speaking so thoroughly that he became the greatest orator of his day.

In any case, I discovered that the angels fly on wings of joy and always act in joy. As they said, *'Joy is what we work with, joy is what we are, what you are. Let us show you this, let us show the whole of humanity.'* They even said:

Throw all conditioning overboard and experience from within. Let the joy roll out and unite you with all life. It is limitless, it sweeps all before it, carrying with it the flotsam and jetsam of all the kingdoms and lifting them up to the One. Of course, there are no words for it; away with words. Unite in joy.

To my protest that I had to live an everyday life in a real world, they replied:

151

What is reality? Is not this communion more real, more alive, more Godlike than your everyday consciousness? Yes, you must live and work in your everyday consciousness, but it need not be so limited. It can include this joy. Like you, we have substance on the dense physical plane, but if you really look, you will see the joy in every leaf, every petal, every colour, every scent. We express this divine reality. You can express it even more than we can.

On one memorable occasion a group of us shared a festival of joy with Nature on Midsummer's Eve, the traditional time for Nature revels. About a dozen of us, including a few sedate elderly people, made our way to Randolph's Leap, where great beeches, granite rocks and rushing, peat-coloured torrents combine to make a powerfully beautiful place. We stopped before entering while Ogilvie, through his close rapport with the nature spirits, formally asked permission for mortals to enter and join the revellers. Permission was granted. The mounting joy which I had definitely felt all day exploded, and I think most of us felt the same way, for we gambolled around like four-year olds — and in circles, like the fairies. We must have been a very funny sight, but that joy had to be expressed. The Landscape Angel even suggested that we could celebrate spontaneously at this time of Midsummer's Eve by a natural attunement to God and Nature. Another seasonal rhythm that man celebrates, Christmas, despite its commercialism, generates sufficient joy to be greatly used by the angels for the betterment of humanity. Certain angelic energies, Christmas angels, seemed to appear just at that time of the year for the purpose of spreading the joy appropriately.

According to the angels, the natural state of life, including humanity's, is one of overflowing joy. With that joy, we can lift all life. True creation comes with a contagious, spontaneous joy — angels couldn't imagine duty or compulsion creating a flower! They wanted us humans to let the energy of joy fertilise us, saying, *'This is our gift, the emphasis that we have for the human race at the moment, and it is far more important than any information we can give to the mind.'*

Purity was another characteristic of the devic world. Purity seems to be a positive accompaniment to clear insight. At first I thought that, naturally, angels were pure, because they had no knowledge of evil; and that is true. Then I realised that even greater purity emerges out of such knowledge. A very old person who has had much of the bitterness, the ups and downs of life, and gained wisdom and humour, has, as well, a purity richer by far than the more obvious and lovable purity of a baby.

When working in the garden one day, I had an overwhelming impression of the purity of the devic realm, which seemed at variance with my filthy hands. The Landscape Angel answered my query:

What is dirt but the very substance of this planet refined through aeons of time, the seed bed of life at the disposal of all and every life, not keeping itself to itself but free and removable for all? That immense purity you feel in us is most applicable to Earth.

The same deva also mentioned that we humans talk of cleanliness being next to godliness and wash earth off, yet we pollute that same Earth with poisons which annul life itself. The devas missed no opportunities to try to expand my awareness.

Another time, when walking in the woods, I felt a tremendous purity from the trees. A tree deva, explaining that this purity emanated from their fine attunement to divine energies, said:

There are some humans who do not like our purity, for it is alien to their usual surroundings, and still others who do not feel purity because they are too self-centred. Those who reach out to us we lift. When you are in our aura and reach into your being, you are lifted because we are in a rhythm of harmony. In fact, we can aid humans to achieve an inward peace. There should always be large areas where trees reign supreme and undisturbed, where we can give solace to you. Such areas would ultimately do much for

153

the healing of nations.

Apart from the healing that the purity and peace of the wilderness brings, purity recognised in anything awakens a response. It is another quality that we share with the devas as we grow.

The angels lived and moved and had their being in a consciousness of the unity of all life. Oneness was a fact which they always expressed strongly to us humans. At first the concept of oneness, with which I agreed as a noble theory, had no relevance for me in practical application. After all, I was myself, separate and distinct from anyone or anything else. The devas began educating me about the inter-relatedness in life by saying:

> *You can see that the frost which appears on a window pane on which you blow your breath on a cold day is part of you, or that the plants which we 'feed' with our radiations are part of us. See also that everything is a different materialisation of one life.*

Having led me to recognise physical inter-relatedness, the devas then said that even if we acknowledge the physical inter-dependence of all life, our derivation from a common Source is our true link. We lose our sense of separation only when we accept and move towards that Source. They warned that we were as likely as not to use our forces against each other until we came close enough to the One to *know* that we are moving on the same path to the same goal. I could accept this, but only mentally, for I still felt myself as a being separate from other beings.

Yet the angels kept on talking of living in the consciousness of one world, a consciousness which we could share. A tree deva tried to broaden my ideas by asking why man should go around in little watertight worlds of his own as if he were the only intelligence, when all around were their worlds, bursting with awareness, full of knowledge and truth of inestimable value. We hear rain and consider it merely as water coming

154

down noisily, quenching the thirst of plants or drenching us. In accepting rain as an inanimate thing, as merely part of a process, we thereby miss the joy of the Spirit of Rain with its broad intelligence and great role in life. What rain could impart to mankind of oneness, and of changing and flowing with the life of the Creator, could be an example to all. We block out these mysteries. The angels continually stressed participation in a wider consciousness, the dynamic drama of the wholeness of life, a real world where *'One is one and many at the same time, where we pass and change and form and re-form and dissolve.'* Shelley, in his poem "The Cloud", shares a similar perception:

> I am the daughter of Earth and Water,
>   And the nursling of the Sky;
> I pass through the pores of the ocean and shores;
>   I change, but I cannot die.

In our sense of separation, according to the devas, we do dreadful things. Our attachment to physical reality, our three-dimensional understanding, our classifying, measuring and separating faculties are illusory from the level where everything functions as united manifestations of one life. On that level, as the Sweet William Deva said:

> *We have true freedom to move on and out of each other's existence with no hindrances. Do you not see that it is the purpose of life to be fully manifesting on the outer levels, and fully united and conscious of Oneness at the same time? That is reality. One life breathes through all. Reverence all life, for it is part of you and you are part of it.*

A being whom I called a Lord of the Elements put the theme of oneness even more strongly, saying:

> *Child of the elements, conscious that you are composed of and part of the elements, rejoice. The world and your bodies were perfected through long ages, so that you could find and express the joy of the Creator in all his manifes-*

tations. Humanity today is destroying itself because it thinks it is separate. How can you possibly think you are separate, how can you possibly not know that when the wind blows it is part of you, that the sun gives to you and is part of you with each sunbeam, that from the water you came and the water joins you all, that without the air you breathe you would not live? How can you be so dense as not to know that if one suffers, the whole consciousness of the Earth partakes of that, and when one rejoices, the whole consciousness knows and rejoices?

We want to din into you all the awareness of Oneness. This concept is being received and interpreted everywhere, but we would stress its practical side, the fact that the bodies of all of you are one with the environment and that you cannot abuse the Earth without harming yourselves.

No, it is not a new message, but humanity doesn't seem to realise that Oneness is not confined to the elevated levels where it puts God, but exists right here now. Disturbing the patterns on Earth, the interplay of natural life, is interfering with the processes of the One and ruining prospects for the future of humanity. We must repeat and repeat the need for man to recognise Oneness. We cannot urge this strongly enough. Do you wonder at the violence of the elements? They will be more violent unless man picks up and acts on this message.

You feel almost sick at the intensity of what I am trying to pass on. Feel at the same time the wonder of the glorious peace behind it, which is a perfection of Oneness, to be felt at all times when you are in tune with the infinite. Then all the elements are pouring forth in joy the essence of what they are, their Oneness. This unity is the goal of life. Love and join with all life, which is part of the Creator and part of you.

The angels, through sharing many impassioned and impressive messages on the subject of the oneness of life, had convinced me of the truth of this concept, but their actions were what made it real. They acted from a consciousness of wholeness. I was first aware of this behaviour when a deva would speak of 'I', and then of 'we'; that is, sometimes it spoke as an individual and sometimes as a group. Such niceties made no difference to it; there was a lack of ego or self-awareness which made it possible for a deva to be itself, or to be the whole, or to be nothing, with equal ease. It cared not who had the stage as long as whatever was necessary was being expressed. Gradually I realised that humans could do the same, not by acting from the oneness of a mass emotional sharing, nor the oneness of mental agreement, but the oneness arising from a sense of responsibility to the whole. This was a revelation to me. I began to see that the devic way of life could be the human way, to see increasingly that the devas were exemplars, a step ahead of us. Of course, any experience that I had of oneness, like becoming a small tree for a second, helped me to understand that however limited I might be, basically I was on the way to becoming increasingly conscious of and even acting from unity, with the promise of universes to share.

Living with Peter, Eileen and the three boys in one caravan had been a constant exercise in achieving unity! However diverse we were in personality, we did have one basic factor: our common dedication to doing the will of God, or flowing with the wholeness of life. However much Peter and I might row, my inner guidance and his guidance through Eileen, though approaching problems from different viewpoints, were always in agreement, and always brought us back to a fresh start. To give an example, Peter and I deadlocked on the name of the booklet containing the messages from the tree devas. I was sure it should be called "Talking Trees"; Peter was even more sure that that was a misleading name which would give the impression that individual trees talked. He wanted a more prosaic title, like "Messages from the Devas of Trees". Zero hour came when Eddie, who was setting up the final copy, had to know — and Eddie would only accept a joint decision. Every time I sought within, the phrase 'talking trees' came to me. I walked over the moors, a sure cure until then for gaining the emotional and mental harmony which led to attunement, but still the phrase 'talking trees' kept coming to me. I knew

Peter was right nine times out of ten. Was I wrong, letting personal preferences cloud the issue? What was I to do? Eddie sat waiting, adamant that we agree. Distraught, I went to Eileen and asked her to seek guidance, a procedure which Peter normally used immediately when any question arose, but in this case he was certain I was wrong. To my overwhelming relief, Eileen's guidance confirmed my own, and then Peter accepted the title that I had been given. So from this and other experiences, I knew the truth of the angelic statement that our conscious oneness with God is the only valid link — and in a group many, preferably all, should have that link, so that we may affirm and confirm each other.

Love, of course, is a living link with everything, with each other and with God. Yet for a long time I was unaware of angelic love. Even when the devas became friends, they were friends, not lovers. Maybe they were not lovers because I was not resonating to love. In any case, I received no messages about love. This puzzled me, and I decided that love was not their strong point. The many strange stories of the fairy world, like "La Belle Dame Sans Merci", or of humans entering and never returning from fairyland, the general tone of untouchability, were explained, I decided, by lack of love in the devic evolution. My view was somewhat confirmed when the angels told me that the quality of compassion was not needed in their realm, since nothing was out of harmony to evoke compassion. Heart qualities, according to them, were better developed in the human line, even though love was the bridge between all kingdoms and they could come closer to me when there was love in my heart. They said, *'Love binds us, because it makes us want to be bound, makes us want to be close to you. In a different way it binds us to our work. Love attracts all creation.'*

Still, over the years I had to revise, slowly, my views of the love of the angels. I realised, for instance, that devic understanding of the word was broader than mine. As the Pansy Deva put it:

We love the rain and the sun and the earth and the air;
perhaps the word 'love' gives you the wrong meaning,

for we are part of the rain and the sun and the earth and the air. In our entirety we are all manifestations of those elements.

This was an all-inclusive love, and one June day the Landscape Angel explained that the natural growth was calling forth more of the protective, life-giving radiations of love, on which everything thrives. This love, shining forth in all directions as from a sun, was also being directed specifically by them. When I asked if humans came in for a share of their love at this time, the angel replied:

Yes, humans come under our jurisdiction in this respect. You, too, need the radiations, in fact need them more than others. But with your free will you either accept or reject them. When open and pulsing with life — which is rare — you are powerhouses of love to all you contact. Generally, you are closed, having cut yourselves off from the whole.

It took eight years for me to appreciate that the lack of love I had felt in the devic world was my own fault, because I had been expecting a personal love to be directed to me and had not risen to a level of impersonal love. Devic love was free for all, too general to be apparent. Appropriately, the Deva of the herb Lovage explained:

It is said that the devic world has no love, and it is true that we do not have the limited or preferential love that humans have. We simply live in love, like fish in water. You isolate love; you pick and choose whom to love. Our realm is a sea of love, for our hearts beat to the greatest love of all, Love itself, and our energies go out to all worlds, as the rain falls on the just and the unjust. We could not blend our consciousnesses if our love were limited. One becomes one with what one loves; this is apparent everywhere. When you love God with all your heart, body, mind and soul, you become one with God and hence with all. When you love only your limited self, you are alone. We know no aloneness.

Of course. Alone on the moors or in the woods, I did not feel alone, because I was loving my surroundings. I was reminded that when I was in love with a person, the whole world seemed new and beautiful, even if it revolved around that one person. The Landscape Angel threw an even more lucid light on my understanding of the vast, impersonal angelic love by asking:

Can you imagine being in love with everyone and every-thing? You could not stand it; it would be too much. But as you grow, that is what will happen. You will become more and more aware of the sea of love in which you live, in which we all partake. At present you find a thousand things to block your awareness of it, but nevertheless you live in it. As too much light blinds, so does too much love, until you become used to it. As you touch more deeply into life, you will experience this love. Now can you imagine that you could live with that all-absorbing rela-tionship? Let your imagination help you to reality.

This imagery was very real to me, but I could not remain in that radiant state of being in love with everything. The familiar feeling of the aloofness of the devic world returned. Another herb deva told me that their complete dedication to the will of God made them seem distant, but that would not be so were I more finely attuned. In trying to analyse this remark, I thought of the pattern of the herb but came no closer to the devic level. Again, the deva said, I was thinking of the surface form; love transcends form. The deva further explained:

Because we are in some ways immaculate, you sometimes find it difficult to draw near. Relax into purity and see that all things are pure, incorruptible — all things, including whatever the lower mind considers impure. That pure essence is at the root of all life, and you will feel happy with it when you roam more freely in our dimensions. Then we and our secrets will be known and familiar.

This teaching stretched my mind, and my awareness of love was growing. The Landscape Angel said that man was beginning to love in a more positive way, with knowledge and verve. But somehow this did not apply to my own living situation. We had become a small group, and as we grew we took on more work. An office had been built, then a sanctuary, then a large community centre. Each of these projects was a remarkable, guided achievement in itself, containing wonderful lessons and examples of successful development on the physical level. This growth ensured that we continued to work so hard through the years that there was no time for relaxation, no time for developing better human relationships. As the Landscape Angel said:

You here have yet to discover what will happen, what will flow, as you put forth the power of positive love for all things. You have been circumscribed in many ways. Because there have been only a few of you, you have had to concentrate in certain directions, and much has been excluded from your love. We have rejoiced that you have included our world up to a point, but we are eager to suggest more avenues for your love. All things have a place and purpose; even stones are patterns of light and have their function, and all creatures come from the hand of the great designer. Humans, bent on their own designs and with little love, have ignored worlds which can now be incorporated into their consciousness.

Remember, we see life in terms of light. We see man becoming alive to his light and linking with humans and with the mineral, vegetable and animal worlds. This is the time of linking, with love, to the light that is everywhere. As you find it in yourselves, you find it elsewhere, and our world will eagerly show you more light as you come to us in love.

I was now very aware of angelic love, and felt the wonder anew when I saw how quickly plants responded to love, as did the devas, or how the pebbles on the beach seemed brighter

161

when seen with loving eyes. The devas themselves seemed to glory in the wonder of love, and said that its relevance on the material level would be increasingly demonstrated, that:

> *We would sing and shout of the miracle of love. How distant we were to you, and how glad to be distant! We felt estranged. Now all that has gone and we actually want to associate with humans. Nothing has actually changed and yet everything is changed, for love is here. We want to act on the love between us.*

Now, with my greater understanding of love, the angels could talk more about it, about man having the choice to create a world with or without love in his personal life. They obviously didn't think highly of the worlds man had created, but they did esteem love, saying:

> *It is the common everyday emotion of love which best links you with us and with anyone or anything. You talk of getting into a rarified state before you tune into us, but when you cease struggling and let love flood your being, our world is yours and you are part of all. Nothing need be separate from you, and you welcome everything into your consciousness.*
>
> *There is much talk of unity. Love brings life and reality to the talk. All sense of strain or limitation goes when you love. You need no knowledge, which often separates you from life. You need no special training; life itself is the training which brings you to love.*

When I asked what to do about a particular person or thing for which I felt no love and couldn't even imagine loving, I was told that there was always some quality to love in every person, thing or situation. When I found and loved that quality, my whole attitude to that person or thing would change, for the positive flow of that speck of love would clear the way for a greater flow, love being a powerful energy.

This was advice that I practised many times, particularly in

162

the office. I would get bored sitting there all day long, seven days a week, typing (we had no time off). I would wish to be anywhere but in an office, would long to be outside in the fresh air or doing something creative instead of typing routine letters. It seemed to me that even peeling potatoes would be a preferable occupation, for then my thoughts could range freely and not be concentrated on typing words correctly. When I became aware of my negative state and remembered devic advice, I would look around for something to love in the office. Almost invariably that something was the cheerful yellow colour of the walls, a colour which I had chosen. Dwelling on the sunshiny yellow would lighten my thoughts, start a positive flow and be the catalyst for seeing other things to love in my surroundings. My resistance to office work continued for thirty years, until I learned to love it and thereby be freed from it; for as long as we hate something we draw it to ourselves.

As love grew in me, it seemed that it grew in the devas and that they were poised with great love towards sympathetic humans. To me their attitude was singularly beautiful, because when angels do anything, even giving a glance, they do it wholly. Unlike humans, they do not have surface hardness from the scars of old wounds or from old shells. They have no reservations. They are forever young and whole, and they call to what is forever young and whole in us. Actually more people, especially young ones, are turning to life with the same beautiful openness, and as the Landscape Angel said:

> *You can respond just as immediately and as freely, as long as surface limitations have not beguiled you. You can let every creature be as new and fresh to you as we are, and then you make spontaneous contact with them and go your way rejoicing. Every soul is beautiful, and each soul responds to love.*
>
> *You need not worry about creating a witless world where everyone floats on pink clouds. The energies that flow through us and all of life are purposeful and forceful. Love is a firm reality forming a bridge over which all can walk. Gooey sentiment is not love, and does not exist with*

us. When we step towards you, we do it energetically; you can do the same. Though you cannot see or hear us, touch, smell or taste us, still we are a tremendous force. We stand here in love, a whole dynamic world ready for an intelligent relationship with an aware humanity. You need us, and we are ready, awaiting the recognition, love and just treatment that you give your own kin. We wait in love for your love.

According to the angels, the dynamism of their world was also innate in humans. Their first message had referred to humans as potential powerhouses. Only Peter expressed power in his person — Eileen and I were too unsure of ourselves — but as group in our first year at Findhorn, we had recognised the angels, asked for their help and then had willingly used our hands, our feet and our brains to apply that help. The tremendous growth of the garden was evidence that some out-of-the-ordinary power was working. The devas said, *'Neither the power within you, nor our power and cooperation, is awakened until it is recognised and evoked. This is only a beginning in this work. You are experimenting and learning, and your faith is growing.'* To me, angelic power was impressive, a sort of stark strength combined with lightness and freedom, an eternal, untouched force behind all their joy.

The devas often talked of human power, the fact that our thoughts gave strength or weakness to plants, that our positive thinking helped keep the garden disease free, or could control the weather. They also discussed psychological ways of encouraging man's effectiveness, for example by our appreciating the good instead of the bad in a situation. The Red Sage Deva, likening the staggeringly quick growth of a plant to the marvellous growth of a human being, made the sage remark that humans can control everything:

You have previously thought that the energies of life are beyond your control except as you manipulate outer form, but as you become aware of and attuned to the energy worlds behind form, and as you learn mastery of the energy patterns which your own thoughts and feelings create, you have all control. As long as you retain your human sense of separation, as long as you think anything in your life is outside of yourself and can blame something or someone for what happens to you, you are in ignorance. You are outside the reality of oneness, and our energy worlds are beyond your ken. When you accept the unity of life, all life is yours and you are all life.

The St. John's Wort Deva talked of one aspect of power used in creation, an aspect ultimately seen in the wonderful delicacy, intricacy and perfection of a plant pattern:

Whatever happens, we hold the archetypal pattern immovable. If alteration is necessary, we hold the alteration as part of the pattern. Then it is unchanging, a great steadiness stemming from the eternal peace of God. The incredible activity of our kingdom clusters around the patterns, making sure that they are brought into form perfectly, serving them endlessly. We state this because we would have you realise that you too have the same quality of undeviating devotion to a pattern, which you can hold in rock-like peace under God.

The deva went on to say that although our higher selves held our individual patterns in steadiness, it was best for our lower minds not to know our destinies, until we were more centred on the divine. Then we could join them in wielding great power. To the angels, our difficulties were due to our lack of contact with our inner strength.

Lastly, a sense of humour was a quality to which the devas gave special priority. Their view of it and their participation in it was unique and bracing:

Flowing through the spheres from the throne of God are many movements, like rivers. There is grace of movement,

*for example, which starts out as a small rhythm and ex-
tends itself to all of life, keeping in touch with beauty.
There is graciousness, which bends itself into your awareness but keeps a close link on high.*

*But we present to you most of all a sense of humour,
which can operate on all levels at once, which bounces
through the universe with the speed of light. Being light
itself, it melts and lifts all it contacts. The devas of fun
have immense scope, with entry where all else fails. They
affect all kingdoms, but in humanity they find fullest
range.*

*It is the greatest privilege to be a deva of this attribute,
to see the most dense darkness become light in a flash and
open a pathway for myriads of our hosts. From the depths
of despair, a smile can appear and a soul feel alive again,
ready for change and movement. Time and place become
nothing. There are no tortuous roads to climb, for an instant touch of humour transports a soul into another
world, a bright hopeful world where anything is possible.*

*We do not tell you what to do; we are not trying to
teach you. We are merely explaining, from our point of
view, the wondrous work of fun. God has created all wonders, but perhaps the most magic one of all is when, from
the most unexpected place, we see a sudden blaze of light
— someone has laughed, and all is well. Negative humans
can switch in a second, smile, and see a way again. Those
who are stuck in routine, those who draw to themselves all
kinds of obstacles, can suddenly see the ridiculous side of
life and thereby be freed.*

*We devas are very busy in this specialised work, darting
from one dimension to another with the greatest of
subtlety. It is the most sensitive art, for each form of life
differs and responds differently to us. We must be ready at
the critical moment to take advantage of the slightest
shift in life's complexities, and be there, entire, to pull the*

166

right lever, so to speak, and let the light in. Where other angles fear to tread we go, forming a network of steady yet instantaneously changing help. And we always enjoy what we do. Much is asked of us. Our reward is great.

So remember, humans, next time something tickles your fancy and brings a different perspective, that God has bestowed on you another of his gifts, perchance through our agency, and rejoice with us in the wonder and meaning of life.

The wonder and meaning of life continued to mix with the tests of life. The devas continued to educate me through sharing the styles and techniques of their living, and I tried to apply these in my life. Their emphasis on acting from a whole consciousness and pure motives was confirmed by two influential new arrivals at Findhorn.

David Spangler, a young new age writer and educator, and his partner, Myrtle Glines, a human relations counsellor, came for a short visit and stayed three years. Immediately, I was able to accept David's very special teaching and energy, and was grateful that he confirmed and experienced angelic reality. Almost always when he gave a talk I would think, 'Of course, I know that. Why didn't I know that I knew?' He obviously drew out my inner knowing. Partly drawn, perhaps, by David's sense of fun, many young people appeared, and the performing arts began. Briefly, during those three years the community growth leapfrogged from about 25 to 200 people and included many new buildings and activities; but the emphasis of David and Myrtle on the importance of consciousness and of relationships counterbalanced the physical growth. They projected a college, and many people, including myself, were attracted to that development. A trial run, with community members and visitors as staff, brought new approaches to spiritual living and broadened the views of old members.

I was still in the office, however, feeling typecast but not knowing how to change my role. Gradually I came to the decision, confirmed by my inner guidance, that it was time for me to leave Findhorn and return to North America. My immediate work lay there; whatever that work would turn out to be, I knew it included writing a book on the angels.

*Our task
is to become
what we are.*

Theodore Roszak

Chapter 11

The Paradox of Personality

I worked on the first draft of this book in the High Sierras of California. There also a group of fifteen of us who had met at Findhorn over the formation of the college, including David Spangler, came together again and decided to work as a group. Eventually we called ourselves the Lorian Association and settled for some years in the San Francisco Bay area.

Our first joint endeavour was to give an afternoon performance of talks, slides, songs and dance about our common spiritual interest, with an emphasis on relating to Nature. I had to speak, and I was terrified. I had had several traumatic experiences in public speaking at my university, including one in which I was literally petrified and had to be forcibly moved. After that I had made no public speeches, but now I knew I must overcome my fear. I memorised my speech, I practised on a tape recorder, and in agony I went out onto the platform with, I am sure, every Lorian member praying for me. The talk, in spite of myself, communicated something to the audience, who gave a considerable response. Some saw angels! I was completely unaware of that, but I had been plugging for them! After that first ordeal, future talks gave me more practice, and I overcame any terror, finding that the audiences, admittedly people interested in the subject, accepted what I said about devas.

When I showed friends the draft of my book, in which I had attempted to arrange and explain the deva messages, without exception they made one comment: 'Put yourself into it.' Put myself into it! I had spent more than half my life trying to get myself out of everything. My training and interest was to be with God and to forget the self. At Findhorn my guidance had sometimes been sought, but not my views. In any case, I was ordinary, with the usual share of flaws. Who would want to read about me? My friends remained adamant, saying that I had to be a human bridge to the angels, as I was when I talked, or only the converted would read the book. But who was this person Dorothy? What part was bookworthy? I shelved writing. Instinctively, I shelved meditation, and let the bubbling, inquisitive life of the Bay Area impinge. My friends continued to treat me as a whole person, not as a sensitive.

I soon perceived that talk of devas or fairies was welcome—as psychic phenomena. But in my contact with the devas, I had to rise to a level of oneness beyond my emotions and thoughts, beyond the astral and beyond psychic phenomena, which had always repelled me anyway. I pondered on the reason for my experiences with the angels and the extraordinary public interest in them. Was it escape? Maybe people were looking for fantasy to shield them from the actualities of the world, or maybe there was something inherent in the devic world and devic contact which is important for man to know now for his survival?

We live in a time of changing orthodoxies. For nearly three hundred years we in the Judeo-Christian West have lived in a society that, by the standards and experience of most historical cultures, would be considered highly unorthodox. We have wrapped ourselves in a world view almost completely derived from science, largely divorced from Nature and with a technological and industrial bent that, placing prime value on what is humanly created, regards the natural environment as little more than a source of raw materials. This mode of separation from the visible and invisible worlds of Nature is unique to our civilisation. Most cultures in human history have believed that all life forms are imbued with a spirit or essence, and that spirit may exist without form, and even precedes and is responsible for the creation of form. That these beliefs reflect a reality has been the experience of countless, perhaps even the majority of, human beings through the centuries.

For example, the Egyptians had a vast array of gods whom they regarded as living beings and as part of their daily lives. In the civilisation of Greece, both the forms of Nature and the various virtues such as courage, wisdom, love and so forth, were considered by many to be the manifestation of ensouling deities. Eastern religions such as Hinduism and Tibetan Buddhism have myriad gods and goddesses who are traditionally worshipped as the manifold aspects of the One. Most tribal societies throughout the world have their presiding deities. The Native American had a particularly intimate and living relationship with the vital forces of Nature, one which was very relevant in his dealing with his environment and the creation of culture. Even our Christian tradition has its angelology.

However, the Jewish and Christian religions have had perhaps the least connection with Nature. Christianity, in its attempts to suppress paganism, took over the festivals of Nature that celebrated and honoured the various gods and overlords of the environment and reinterpreted them in terms of Christian dogma, often separating these festivals from their original symbolism and connection with Nature. This disconnection from Nature has significantly contributed to the development of our present unorthodox society, governed by a materialistic world view which ignores any possibility of a spiritual presence or presences in the forms that surround us, and treats Nature as something separate from ourselves which we must dominate, rather than as an organism of which we are a part and with which we must commune and cooperate. One result of this unorthodox-become-orthodoxy is our increasingly polluted and disrupted ecology, with all its attendant dangers and threats to the continuance of the rich and diverse patterns of life on this planet.

However, the world of the angels, and all its energy for abundant life and creativity, is still available to us, and in recent years more attention and acceptance is being given to it. Our orthodoxies are changing again, and a place like Findhorn, which is based on communication with spiritual presences, or a person like myself, are both being given credence. The gods are coming to life again.

But why were the gods coming to life in our time, just when they had been satisfactorily explained away as archetypes of the collective unconscious, as productions and projections of the human psyche? The common inherited biology of man was said to account for the astonishing similarity of myths throughout the world. Therefore, myths were no longer considered fantasy, but veiled explanations of truth, helpful to man to guide him step by step through the psychological crises of life. To me these explanations were true and helpful, but myths also have other levels of meaning and application.

Perhaps a reason for the reappearance of the gods was that the probing mind of man had done away with superstition and largely broken the power of a horrendous image 'out there' which could manipulate his life. Now that man recognises himself as part of the power that creates his world, he can deal directly with another spiral of truth: the angelic realities which originally gave rise to his mythic images. The fact that the angels, the devas, the gods, live on a level different from the physical is quite enough for us to regard them as beings to be appealed to, placated, worshipped and feared. Now that we know that we also share that devic level, that we too have creative power, that we too (though not yet with the wisdom of the gods) can control our world, we can deal with the devas as equals; fellow sojourners and learners on this planet and on other realms. We too are cosmic beings and, as such, no longer need fear either Nature or the gods, but can accept them as having different but complementary parts to play on this earth.

As we learn to function with our higher consciousness, we take over the destiny of the planet. As a Lord of Evolution said:

174

I have shaped your vehicles from a wonderful blend of the elements, and have lovingly fashioned your unique expressions of life. Now I can hand this task over to those of you who accept your wholeness. You have all you need to create new patterns and new dimensions of life on this planet and beyond. This is your tremendous responsibility.

Another deva said that the human who is master of his or her personality is a shining being to whom the angelic ranks go for strength and love.

Such a human is the climax of our work on this planet, such a human has power in all worlds. To these ones all reverence; they are Lords of the Planet and of all they survey, the wisdom of the ages and the light of the futures.

However, humanity is not yet at the stage where it is the light of the world. We still seem bent on exploiting, if not downright destroying , our planet. Are the angelic presences relevant to us in our present state? It seemed to me that awareness of the reality of the angels of Nature, with the possibility of cooperation from them, could not have come at a more opportune time.

I can remember when the use of 24D brought innocent glee to the face of my father because it killed the weeds but not the grass of his lawn. In the thirty years since — in half a lifetime — the biological balance of the world has been upset. Increased concentrations of harmful substances are in our foodstuffs, breathing is difficult, rivers and lakes have become sewers and even the oceans are polluted, while many species of animals and birds are in danger of extinction. According to Professor J. W. Forrester of the Massachusetts Institute of Technology, the changes occurring in our generation have been as great as those in the previous 2,000 generations.

The past can no longer act as our guide. Though, technologically, we are able to make still vaster changes in our environment, we lack sufficient knowledge to assess in advance the consequences of our actions. In the opinion of Professor Forrester, man's intellectual powers are quite inadequate for unravelling the finely tangled net of interrelationships in our modern social system. The evolutionary process has failed to provide us with the mental powers needed for correct interpretation of the systems to which we ourselves belong, and for the time being all attempts to plan mankind's future with any degree of accuracy are useless. The Aswan Dam is an example of the truth of his statements. It seems that angelic cooperation, with humans using the supramental powers of the angelic level of our beings, may give us the only answer to the mess that we have created.

But, from any level, acceptance that there is an intelligence behind everything, that we and our natural environment share similar areas of consciousness, that everything responds to love and laughter, that we can have a two-way communication with whatever beings we think of, all this brings a new fullness and meaning to life. We need no longer act as isolated units; we can join in universality. We can serve and help the Earth itself. We can acquire a new sense of destiny.

Man had considered that some overarching purpose ruled the world until thinkers like Galileo and Newton helped create the idea that the workings of Nature could be explained as mechanisms. To the scientific mind, the laws and principles of motion and matter were forces not needing the hypothesis of God as Creator. Darwin's discoveries in biology gave the same message even more strongly. We in the West have accepted these principles, to the extent that our individual worlds have also become purposeless.

Now psychologists have begun to discover the value of a felt sense of purpose. Carl Jung found that people became neurotic when their lives did not have sufficient content, sufficient meaning, but that neuroses generally disappeared if these people were able to develop into more spacious personalities. Abraham Maslow found that, without exception, self-actualising (acting with all of themselves, complete, integrated) people were dedicated to some work, duty or function which they considered important. Because they

176

were interested in their work and found it exciting and fulfilling, they worked hard and the usual distinction between work and play became blurred. The devas too made no distinction between work and play.

Maslow also considered that it was not enough to have an important job; the self-actualising person must do it well, which often involved hard work, discipline, training and postponement of pleasure. To Maslow, the ultimate disaster of our times is valuelessness. Jung also found, when visiting the Native Americans of the Pueblo tribes, that their dignity and tranquil composure sprang from their belief in being sons of the Sun and helping the Sun across the sky. This gave their lives cosmological meaning. It is not knowledge that truly enriches us; we need something more. If we are not bound by some conviction, conscious or unconscious, about the significance of life, we drift. It is not enough to know that kindliness is good and that cruelty is bad. Yet we do need the will to good, and that lies within our power.

Well, I had the will to good; why was I not a self-actualised being? Like Paul, the good that I would I did not. The problem of good and bad kept recurring in my life. My search had not ended with Christian teachings. My next teaching, that of Hazrat Inayat Khan, helped me to realise that right and wrong are often artificial standards, varying in each country, which seem outwardly to create moral law but in the end cause degeneration. Yet every child has a natural sense of right and wrong, for a child *feels* a wrong vibration; it is adults who become confused. Inayat Khan believed that man should be taught to consult his own spirit and from his own feelings find and make the distinction between right and wrong, good and bad. If this natural principle were adopted by humanity, perhaps the greater part of the world's misery would come to an end. Spirit alone has the right to discern between right and wrong. He said that we have to experience sorrow and suffering on the way, because in order to find goodness one must find wickedness for comparison—that we have to experience pain *and* pleasure, as everything is distinguished by its opposite. According to Inayat Khan, evil and ugliness, which are the

177

shadows of goodness, 'exist' in man's limited conception but are in actuality as non-existent as shadows. The 'impression' of sin, the *imprint* over the purity of the soul, is a form of mental illness, for in reality there is no sin, no virtue, that can be engraved on the soul. These can only cover the soul, whose essence is divine intelligence. If we trust in goodness, evil, the shadow, will disappear.

All these teachings helped to lighten my shadows and still, today, contain truths for me. That our greatest difficulties are our best opportunities is a truth that I have proved again and again in my own life. I remember being told in a horoscope reading that, during a certain period of my life, everything had been against me and I would not have been nice to know then. Yet that difficult period was when I made my first real spiritual step, that of acting with unselfish love in my marriage.

It is our problems that compel us to seek *spiritual* good, otherwise we would not rise above the level of being good human beings. It was delightful to read that William Blake, probably alone among his contemporaries, had a similar view: 'Without Contraries is no Progression. Attraction and Repulsion, Reason and Energy, Love and Hate, are necessary to Human existence.' Ram Dass states that despair is the necessary prerequisite for the attainment of the next level of consciousness. Alan Watts cast his usual witty light on the subject when he said that in Buddhist countries, where everything that happens to you is understood as your own karma, you have no one to blame but yourself when things go wrong. You are not a sinner but a fool, so try another way.

But, to me, some Far Eastern teaching, in treating this world as illusion, as maya, can create an even deeper split in our attitude to life. I had neither an inclination toward nor experience of such a view. Once when I was wandering the moors at Findhorn, I had a vast realisation of the divinity of the wonderful natural cover of the earth and my body and its instincts being all in the same category. There is infinite wisdom in our instinctual drives, in our desire for food or sex. It is not the body that is greedy, bad or perverted, it is the mind.

178

It is not animals that kill wantonly, it is man. In fact, as our minds recognise and value our intuition or our devic selves, we can welcome back and listen to the innate wisdom of our bodies. As Walt Whitman said in "I Sing the Body Electric": 'If anything is sacred, the human body is sacred.'

Abraham Maslow had interesting things to say on the subject of good and bad. He found that mature people had little struggle between good and bad, as they consistently chose and preferred the better values. The dichotomy between good and bad was present only in more average individuals who were not consistent with themselves. Real guilt, which he considered a result of a person's failure to live up to his potential, had a useful function because it could direct a person toward personality growth. The free choice of self-actualising, healthy, normal people tells us what is good and bad, and these choices are essentially the same around the world.

In **Sources**, Theodore Roszak has written:

> Reason/feeling, mind/body, state/society, man/nature, all the dichotomies are in essence one: a distrust of spontaneous process, a need (born out of fear) to petrify and dominate, an incapacity to be easy and swing with the given rhythm. . . . All the dichotomies work to establish invidious hierarchies. Reason, Mind, State, Man become boss-big-shot, top-dog, headquarters, command-and-control-center. Feeling, body, society, nature must then play nigger: bow, scrape, cringe, obey and serve in total abasement. All the dichotomies end in disaster. For the Tao, being infinitely elastic, may bend, but will never break, and at last restores the balance—somehow. Eventually, the bottom dogs reclaim their own. Feeling rebels as nightmare, Body rebels as ulcer, heart attack, asthma, migraine; the psychosomatics. The rebellions draw blood; they are nonetheless a summons to health. All the dichotomies yield to an identical therapy: the restoration of wholeness. Reason and feeling made one become the person. Mind and body made one become the organism. State and society made one become community. Man

and nature made one become ecology.

The restoration of wholeness was the constant theme of the angels. They also stated that these opposites had the function of making man emerge from unknowingness into consciousness of wholeness. I have written that the angels are above the pairs of opposites. By this I meant that their qualities were of the realm of wholeness, that they did not attach value to these opposites, and they did not judge. Much of form or creation emerges out of the relationship between complementary opposites or polarities, and of course the devas use this principle in creation. We humans, living in a morphic world, a world of form, still need values, our individual versions of what is good and bad, so that we may continue to choose and move to new values.

Choice is essential. Our superiority stems from our retaining the freedom of choice, remaining universally adaptable and so generalists in a world of specialists. One does not resist evil, because everything that comes to us is drawn for some purpose, and resistance, while it brings pain, provides no cure. Neither should we condone our evils, but rather seek to understand ourselves and to choose to extend our identity into the wholeness of our being. We can only flow with the Tao when we are one with it, without desire, functioning fully with our angelic selves. As Roszak put it in Unfinished Animal:

> The psychotherapy of the future will not find the secret of the soul's distress in the futile and tormenting clash of instinctual drives, but in the tension between potentiality and actuality. It will see that, as evolution's unfinished animal, our task is to become what we are, but our neurotic burden is that we do not, except for a gifted few among us, know what we are.

Yes, we must know what we are. Recognition is the path to Christ. We only attempt to do something when we believe that we have the capability to achieve it, just as I did not attempt to contact angels until I was in the state to believe that

180

it was possible. The devas kept telling me about our capabilities, about what we are: gods in the making, possessors of infinite potential, one with them in the angelic realm. This oneness with the angels might be described in psychological terms by quoting from Irene Claremont de Castillejo's Knowing Woman:

> Most children are born with, and many women retain, a diffuse awareness of the wholeness of nature, where everything is linked with everything and they feel themselves to be part of an individual whole. It is from this layer of the psyche which is not yet broken into parts that come the wise utterances of children. Here lies the wisdom of artists, and the words and parables of prophets, spoken obliquely so that only those who have ears to hear can hear, and the less mature will not be shattered.

This, to me, was a good description of the area of my own consciousness which blended with the devic consciousness. I had often wondered why contacting angels had fallen to my lot, and the only connection that I had ever found was that I, when alone with Nature, was blissfully in tune with everything. In de Castillejo's Jungian book this area was roughly observed as that of feminine consciousness, a diffuse awareness, as opposed to the masculine consciousness, a focused consciousness. Of course, the makeup of all human beings includes both these consciousnesses, but generally speaking, diffuse awareness is more common in women. Women on the whole are more concerned with life's relationships, men with the hows and whys of various aspects of life. Both approaches are inadequate without the other, for vague intuitions are dreamy nothingnesses until concretely applied; yet concrete applications without a sense of wholeness have brought our world into its present dilemmas. The feminine half of the individual and of mankind has been in subjection to the masculine half, and is only now beginning to be liberated.

Ms. de Castillejo, in writing that the persistent inner voice of women is 'You are no good', helped me to realise that this was true for me, that I had denied part of myself. She

181

explained that this judgment of ourselves was the outcome of man's collective unconscious fear of woman's rivalry and his passionate desire to keep her in her place. But it is more than that; it is also the desire of the mind to dominate, a phase necessary for the development of the mind. During this phase mankind has denied its devic consciousness, its diffuse awareness, and of course women have felt this most. But now we can claim our birthright and see the worth of our 'feminine' values instead of adopting the values of the intellect.

I do not mean to imply that angelic consciousness is not focused. Obviously it is, in the holding of archetypal patterns until these are translated into the infinite yet exacting details of form, in the perfection of a flower or a body. But the angels, unlike humanity, in their focusedness never lose their sense of the whole.

Because of inner guidance almost twenty-five years ago, I had tried not to follow the values of the intellect in my life and had concentrated on the 'higher' values. I had not been all that successful. I now realise that most of the clashes that I had with Peter Caddy were because some course of action of his had challenged my diffuse awareness, yet when confronting him I had used mental arguments. In context my arguments were generally nonsensical, aggravated by my upset emotions and by my unawareness of what I was doing. But as we learn to esteem the awareness of oneness and take our standards from there, the indispensable mind can be used to apply our vision wherever necessary. Then the mind, no longer master, can find its true place in the wholeness of ourselves and of the world, using its gift of formulation to express the wisdom of the level of diffuse awareness.

In this kind of achievement, artists and humanity's great spiritual teachers have been supremely important. Creative artists have always managed to keep contact with devic consciousness, in spite of being brought up in a society based on focused consciousness. Artists have a great capacity to express the whole of their personalities and therefore their contribution to humanity has been of great significance. William Blake, recognising this, laid tremendous emphasis on art, and believed that imagination was a high order of force that could overcome other forces, and that art was the language of the imagination. I believe people from all walks of life are now emerging to begin expressing the whole of their personalities in their own particular fields.

In the present state of the world, the necessary component of life on the planet is awareness of wholeness with regard to Nature and ourselves, an awareness with which women are often more familiar and in tune. But women must learn to focus and give priority to what we find valid in our own experience without need to look to the past for justification. The close relationship of a poet or mystic to Nature can be everyone's ordinary relationship, and our culture changed from one of rapism to one of interchange with and appreciation of the beauty and value of the Earth and beyond. One way that we men and women can cease splitting ourselves into various parts, even cease dichotomising being and becoming, is to recognise our androgynous wholeness. Here again the angels are an example. Androgynous, they use their masculine and feminine aspects as suits the situation.

It is from our wholeness, our divinity, that we can then relate to anyone else and to our world. If I am out of tune with myself, I am out of tune with the universe. The core of relationship is to be at one with oneself and therefore at one with the essence of everything. The devas gave me invaluable help, because in contacting them I had to go through the process of expanding to my own essence, my soul. Just as the outer form of a human being indicates its essence, its soul, its core, so the outer form of a garden pea indicates its essence, its soul (in this case a group soul). The same process of expanding to our own essence is necessary for a true relationship, one not limited by appearances, with *anyone*.

The devas said that the paradoxes of our personalities were our concern. They could give many clues, as in helping me to become aware that I habitually chose to limit myself. However, because of the clarity of their realm and their lack of choice, it is our prerogative, as humans, to be the bridge between worlds:

You can say that the human ability to bridge arises from tensions, polarities; you can say that it arises from innate growth mechanisms, or from divine discontent, or that you include all probabilities, or, as you feel it with us, as just energy of loving joy beyond the pairs of opposites, which simply contains all and which is often called God, or life, the core of everything. Of this we sing, and the siren song of the self also ultimately sings the same song, for as you know yourself you know everything. So embrace whatever life brings, knowing that it comes as a gift of that great joy, to draw you to itself. Through it you emerge as a personality as beautiful as a flower, as powerful as any natural force, as expansive in its love as the reach of the sun, as creative as Nature itself. Then it is not you and I, it is we together in the life we share.

The period of studying and writing and being in California has brought this small town, conservative Canadian to an acceptance of even being androgynous. No one knows better than the small town girl that I am not there yet, but my angelic self knows deeper things — and the two of us not only no longer fight but have lost the twoness. For a period, when consciously trying to tune into my divinity, I was instantly aware of that great Presence within me. Then I was humbled yet glorified, and a few tears would course down my cheeks, to the dislike of my unemotional self. Now, after a deep experience of the unity of my so-called higher and lower selves, I can love my personality and see it in its true light as the indispensable vehicle that every human needs for life's fullest expression, as the chosen instrument of one's soul. The long journey continues, but I have learned to relax in the present, knowing that whatever comes is part of my ongoing, to be welcomed, learned from, enjoyed. And the paradoxes continue to provide the spice.

It is not by wanting
to experience another realm
that we get there,
but by being completely aware of every action,
every sound and colour around us,
every relationship.

Chapter 12

Humans and Angels Now

Angels, then, show us our future, though they would not use that term. To them the future is contained within the present. Though we do not always perceive it, we are whole beings now, and must accept what we are. However, as the angels have not come via our human path, they cannot serve as a sign-post labelled 'This is the way, for we have trodden it.' But the planet has many way-showers. Many great teachers, religious or otherwise, have walked the Earth, and from each one we can learn. Yet the angels, from their vantage point and from their interplay with our consciousness, can see what we truly are, can see the steps in front of us, and continue to help us connect to our divine origin and goal. Now we can consciously seek their cooperation. The creative living styles described in Chapter 10 are both the way leading to the angels and the way they, the angels, are becoming and being. Joy, love, flexibility, freedom, harmony are what we are, the essential nature of all life — but we humans have to know it. We simply have not known what we are; but clearly, beautifully, the devas spelt it out for me, shared with me what I am. They said it in the conscious communion that I developed with them, until I became aware that the same message was conveyed in Nature, in every particle of life.

Every flower is shouting at us of our common divinity, of our transcendent selves. We know it unconsciously. Our paradises have been gardens. We 'say it with flowers.' Our symbolic pictures of the universe, our mandalas, are flower designs. But now flowers are saying, with a new intensity, 'Look, don't think; look directly at us and see God.' Our minds may translate the call as 'Look at our colour, at our design, at our intricate delicate beauty.' Their fragrance joins in the same message: 'Breathe in my scent; that too is of God.' The touch of the grass, of a pebble, of wood, of running water, of sun, also exclaims: 'Touch me, feel me, I am a wonderful life for you to blend with, to admire or carve or shape, and I too am divine.' Our very taste buds distinguish delectable flavours and we savour yet another creation of the whole, another expression of God. Sound, natural or manmade, can lift us to harmony, and then leave us in the silence necessary for the thunder of God.

We have caught up with Blake's vision of wholeness: 'Man has no Body distinct from his Soul, for that called Body is a portion of Soul discern'd by the five Senses, the chief inlets of 'Soul in this age'. Even Karl Marx, in his early speculations, called for the resurrection of human nature, for the human physical senses to be emancipated from the sense of possession, and then humanity, free of the domination of the senses, could enjoy them for the first time. I believe this is what Krishnamurti says when he urges us to watch Nature without thought, without judgment, without wanting to continue the joy, because when thought takes over the joy, it becomes pleasure, mechanistic, back in the round of pleasure/pain. It is not by wanting to experience another realm that we get there, but by being completely aware of every action, every sound and colour around us, every relationship. Or, as don Juan said, apprehending the world without interpretation, with pure wondering perception.

Through the senses and minds of mankind, a clod of earth talks of the millennia of its history, of the myriad invisible lives contained within it, of the manifold visible life that grows from it. The animals speak directly through their incredible grace and instinct, birds through song or their unerring migrational flights. Man talks most of all and with greatest complexity! Hidden behind his speech is a being whose glance can mean heaven or hell to another, a being who can be judged as ennobling, degrading or anything we like. A strange, powerful creature whose touch of individual spirit is ever beyond knowing. A miracle. 'What is man, that thou are mindful of him . . . Thou has crowned him with glory and honour. Thou madest him to have dominion over the works of thy hands . . . O Lord our God, how excellent is thy name in all the earth!' (Psalm 8)

Although man is a miracle, to many the flower is a more compelling expression of perfection. So perhaps it is easiest, through awareness of flowers in particular, of their radiant beauty and purity, their uncomplicated stillness, their vibrant colour, to come to the excellence of the One and be uplifted beyond thought to our devic selves. We see white spring blossoms bursting from a grey stick, and we know that Nature is the glory of God. 'There is one holy book, the sacred manuscript of nature, the only scripture that can enlighten the reader.' (Inayat Khan) To me, with eyes open or closed, tuning into the essence or beauty of any wild place is heaven. And that glory is infinitely enhanced by knowing that we can relate to it in the realm of consciousness, that we can unite with and translate its intelligence, since we are the same intelligence.

Of course, Nature does not speak in the same language to everyone, and can even bring fear to some. And God cannot be heard by those whose every effort is directed toward finding the next meal. Still, a mathematical equation may awaken the soul of a mathematician. The arts, which are a blend of devic and human energies, may speak most clearly to many of us, through a Gothic cathedral, a painting, a poem, a ballet or, most universally of all, through music. A smile, a sexual experience, or an athletic achievement may give us a transcendent experience. With a sense of wonder, something in our environment uplifts our whole being, and we are more whole than before.

We are all wayfaring to our future. We have in common, as Goethe said, 'the constant striving upwards, wrestling with oneself, the unquenchable desire for greater purity, wisdom, goodness and love.' That means effort, and perhaps heartache.

189

Although our innate desires will bring us to our future, we can save ourselves a lot of grief by relating *now* to our future, to our devic selves, as well as to our transcendent experiences. In fact, we are continually doing that and always have been, but we were not aware of it. Consciousness of this ability not only makes us relate more concretely to the whole of ourselves, but to the whole of our surroundings. In all we do we can recognise that we belong to a great universe of life. We can apply our relatedness to everything, and we, and everything, become more alive.

Take, for instance, our technology: There is nothing wrong with technology, only the way we apply it. Technology is destructive only in the hands of fragmented, over-specialised people who do not realise that they are one and the same process as the universe. However complicated machinery may be, approaching it, or anything, in the spirit of divine wholeness is relevant. I have recounted my experience with the deva of the offset litho machine at Findhorn, and we had other experiences. For instance, the singing group, the New Troubadours, when trying to record a tape had constant trouble with the various pieces of equipment. Just as everything seemed perfect, one or other of the numerous units would break down. Not until each person concerned had recognised the need to evoke a 'higher' energy was a successful recording achieved.

Of course, this approach could give rise to a cute cult that appeals to the deva of this or the deva of that for everything. That would miss the point, which is that we first recognise and act from our own wholeness, and then from that point of consciousness relate to the similar consciousness in our surroundings. The angels that we encounter in this process are not little kitchen pixies come to clear up our messes. We can only recognise a mess without because it is part of our experience within. Only our whole selves, with the aid of the angels, can untangle our confusions and create a new world. By broadening our view, we change our lives and become more aware of life everywhere, even of the beauty in a rusted tin can. In fact, the power that is increasingly available through science and technology is an agent of change, because of its very vastness. We have to learn the responsible use of technology as an instrument of love. We can begin by caring for and appreciating our tools, our knives, pins or scissors.

In North America we must, in fact, reclaim the heritage of the Continent, a heritage which we have almost destroyed. Whatever our backgrounds, we will not be truly American or Canadian or Mexican until we, like the native peoples, recognise the Earth as our mother, and show respect for every form, function and power of Nature. To the Native Americans, Nature was indeed a holy book of profound value, and though I do not think that we need revive their rituals, the shamanistic veneration for life is essential. Other cultures were similar. As Edward Hymans wrote in Sources:

> For the ancient farmers, and even for those not so far from us in time, every plant and animal and stone and the very Earth herself was alive and animated by spirit. And since, from self-knowledge, man knew that mind and matter, soul and body must be in harmony, in order that the whole should function, he also knew that in manipulating the body of the living world, he must be at one with the spirit animating it.

No civilisation has manipulated the environment as much as the modern North American; no civilisation needs the Native American heritage more than we do.

This fact was once clearly illustrated for me in the San Francisco Bay area. When attuning to the devas in a wild valley there, I found them in a state of shock. This was incredible! Never before or since have I encountered them in other than a high free state. Evidently, the rapid and continuing encroachment of the white man, whose huge machines brutally and thoughtlessly attacked the landscape, was responsible for their state. In Europe, environmental change has come about more gradually through the generations, with a certain rapport between man and Nature. In parts of Scotland, tenant farmers still contract to put manure back onto the land, and to cultivate it on a four-year crop rotation basis. But in America, where

191

man once had such a close relationship with Nature, the white man has taken over with complete indifference to the value of the environment except as something for his own use. It might even be that much of the violence we experience in America is a karmic result of the violence with which we have treated the land. And perhaps those devas that I had encountered in the lovely unspoilt valley had been upset because they had foreseen the machines that would be at work in the valley a year later.

In most ancient societies trees were not wantonly felled, because each tree was believed to possess a soul, and these beliefs were, in fact, effective soil conservation regulations. We need a modern equivalent; and the devas can provide it.

The devas can also provide conscious cooperation with humans who seek their aid from holistic motives. They will cooperate in annulling the destruction man has inflicted on the planet, as we play our part. They will cooperate in joint creative efforts to improve the plant life that they have already created, with hybrids and new experiments, as we play our part. They will cooperate with scientific ecologists in ways yet to be developed. We can each start to play our part by being more considerate in simple ways. We can plant shrubs that grow to a height of five feet when we wish a five foot hedge, instead of planting trees that have to be clipped each year to prevent them attaining their normal fifty feet. We can stop using poisons and start using natural fertilisers. I think our eating habits will eventually change, as we realise the truth of the devic statements that there is more nutrition in small 'natural' vegetables and fruits than in large, chemically treated produce.

For humans, for angels, for all planetary life, wilderness areas are necessary. Nature forces are at their strongest and purest where thinking man has not interfered. I found, for example, more power in a little wild violet in the sand dunes than in the most cosseted garden flower (see Appendix, p. 209). We humans, creators of comparisons leading to the divisions of good and evil and to the development of wisdom, with minds that have cut us off from our souls, need places free of materialistic concepts, free of comparing thoughts, for the restoration of that soul. In addition, the angels need places free of humans. When I flew over the Arctic, devas told me that even the empty frozen wastelands were necessary for certain planetary work. The tree devas have stressed the important role of the forests in helping men and women to find their balance. Every little garden is better off with an area untouched by humans, where the nature spirits can be uninhibited. And, of course, wild animals need wilderness. To be good stewards of the harmonious allotment of the natural resources of this closed system called Earth, we need to use our angelic intelligence as well as our trained minds.

In regard to animals, here again we can learn from the Native American, to whom each animal reflected a particular aspect of the Great Spirit (man reflected all aspects). The Native American believed that knowledge of his oneness with the universe and all its powers could not be realised unless there were perfect humility, unless man humbled himself before the entire creation, before the smallest ant, realising his own nothingness. Only in being nothing can man become every-thing, and only then will he realise his own essential brother/sisterhood with all forms of life. His centre, or life, is the same centre of life of all that is. And our brother/sisterhood from such a centre is a vital link between the different forms of life. A case in point is that of the rats who, at my request, did not disturb me for four years. After that experience I felt a loving link with rats, which they seemed to reciprocate; it might have been my imagination, but it was a constructive imagination based on reality. To have that sort of relationship with all life is a wonderful vision, one that I think appeals to all lovers of life, and it is not impossible. We are all ultimately St. Francises, especially now that we realise that men, not animals, are the villainous destroyers of life on Earth. When we communicate with our pets as equals, not talking down to them, we get a deep response. An attitude of respect, of knowing that all life has a place, is imperative. Unless we wish all wild animals to become extinct and tame animals to be further exploited (and ourselves thereby lessened), it is up to us to exercise our dominion, not against but for the animal world.

Instead of forcing the creation of disease resilient insects by our chemical sprays, we can have a cooperative exchange. As a beekeeper, for instance, I enlisted angelic help, tuning into a wonderfully wise Being who, above all, told me to be peaceful in my handling of the bees, to study and harmonise with the bee ways and then follow my own feelings. My subsequent treatment of them resulted in a honey yield greater than that of others in the area—apart from the joys and sharp sorrows of relating to these fascinating insects.

Regarding humanity, we have many great teachers to show us the way to our future. Do the devas add anything new, anything to help us relate to each other? Yes, in their complete freedom to live wholly. In great living teachers we may glimpse feet of clay, but the devas all have winged feet. That is no criticism; to err is human and often that which we find lovable about human beings is precisely their imperfections. Precisely because so many erring humans are now attuning to their own Christhood, it is nice to have an archetype supplied by the angels. Example can still be helpful.

At least I found angelic example helpful. I would ask myself, for instance, if angels were humble. Not a bit of it; they gloried in their power. Then were they egotistical? Never. They gloried in God and each other. I do not see why humans eventually cannot attain the same state, which, idealistic or not, is the avowed purpose of man's highest endeavour, formalised in all religions. In the present state of the world, in this time of pervasive disclosure of human misdeeds and selfish actions, in this time of the very breakdown of society, we are not in danger of becoming idealists or losing the common touch, but we are in danger of completely losing sight of our angelic selves. We need to re-value ourselves, to recognise our feminine 'diffuse awareness' and focus our consciousness according to its holistic views. As various modern thinkers are pointing out, this is already happening in certain areas here in North America, which is still, for better or worse, a world exemplar. To fulfil the American destiny, to make real the statement that 'We hold these truths to be self-evident, that all men are created equal,' we have to look to our angelic selves. (Obviously, we are not all equal on other levels.)

A devic approach new to humanity is that they learn without suffering. Suffering has been our human way. The First Noble Truth of Buddhism is that all life is sorrowful. The Second Noble Truth is that sorrow is caused by attachment, and the Third Noble Truth is that the release from sorrow comes through giving up attachment. This release is called nirvana. Many people believe that nirvana is this world itself, just as it is, when experienced without desire and fear. I believe, also, that we can be as free as the devas in this world if we function with all our capabilities. Looking back on my life, suffering was, admittedly, the spur that drove me to seek within, but I no longer wallow in misery, anguish in indecision, or look for some panacea or drug. Now I attune to myself to discover purposes and actions.

Consciousness is the knowing faculty. When consciousness has no object to be conscious of, it is pure intelligence. If we believe that we have no intelligence or love, we cut them out of our worlds. How can we be loved if we carry the thought that everyone who sees us dislikes us? We are our own worst enemies. I know that I create my own world, and while I can still suffer in it, not being able to blame anything or anyone else does negate emotional and mental stress and turns me to the area where I can make effective change: myself. The very energy of asking for help from Christ, God, Allah, the angels, is a catalyst for change and is as strong as the strength of my belief. This is not new teaching; but what is so marvellous is the refreshing, magnetically joyful and light approach of the devas.

If the angels bring anything new, it is the quality of joy— appropriate now, because humanity is at the stage where we can express joy in ourselves as we make that giant step from intellect to intuition and leave behind the days of martyrdom and suffering. The devas would point out some shortcoming of mine in such a lighthearted way that I could see it impersonally and not be bound by my error.

195

It has taken years for the belief that I draw to myself all that happens to me to become an integral part of my living. At present we seem to need time and constant realignment to become accustomed to our vastness and to bridge the gaps in ourselves. We continue to make excuses for ourselves, and until we truly see that our own thoughts and memories, both cultural and individual, are behind all our acts, they will continue to fragment us. Our minds will fight to retain their familiar supremacy until we admit that direct perception, higher attunement, transcendence, intuition, or whatever we call it, is valid. Then we can begin to link with all of ourselves and change the way we live.

The devas suggested customary approaches or teachings, which we humans do not yet seem to apply, like being loving, thinking affirmatively, using our energies positively, attuning to inner peace for protection at all times. If we respond to chaos and suffering, we are stuck on that level, stuck to the old, separated, departmentalised world. Let go of the mind and let joy explode! To some people such an approach may appear, not only as an ostrich view of life, but inhumane, narcissistic, unrealistic. They are right, if we cut ourselves off from any part of life. We *are* our society. We have to discover where we fit in, have to be true to ourselves and follow the leads that life gives us. Let others who are much better cooks feed the starving millions; for my part, I am more likely to find, on some level of consciousness, a secret for better food production.

The constant devic reference to life as movement, as energy, as change, is in keeping with our fast modern world. The old static codes and moralities are dead shells. Yet the eternal value of goodness still applies, and those who break it for power or material success find, even in this lifetime, destruction, not fulfilment. Modern titans, such as the corporate oil companies, could follow the same self-destructive path unless, like the power-controlling devas, they serve the whole. We can no longer deny the inter-relatedness of life. But we can, like the devas, blend with the new waves of energy we encounter as we live in harmony with that still small voice within, doing the best that we know in our circumstances. As we attune to our divinity, all creation attunes to us. We find our acts bear fruit, that a book opens at the page containing the answer we seek, or that the very person we need suddenly turns up. We ride the crest of the wave, until the natural rhythm of our life takes us through the hollow to another crest. We start generating more subtle energy. In the whirling devic forces problems vanish, as we see solutions from that level. Our finest thoughts become powerful enough to take form on Earth, in new relationships, in a garden, in the arts.

The first step in cooperation with a new dimension is to choose it, which is another way of saying 'I believe' or 'I know'. We humans are strange mixtures; while we do not believe that we are the gods that the devas say we are, nevertheless we act like gods. We have been true pagan deities on this planet, taking for granted that we have sole control of it, yet not invoking our divinity. While we gayly admit the devil in us, we are ashamed to admit the god in us. The angels say that it is high time that we know what we are, and join our warring parts together. Disillusionment is a good clean starting point. Only in unity can we, and the whole Earth, survive. As we realise our basic oneness with all life, we appreciate our differences more. First we have to attune to our uniqueness, our part of the vastness, our Godhood, before we can know and work with it, and from that growing awareness mingle with others in this diverse world.

The devas have made it easier for me to link up with my fellow man. Having learned that behind the so-called 'stupid' green vegetable is a lively intelligence, I can more readily acknowledge a lively intelligence behind the pitted face of my fellow human or the one I see in the mirror. As the angels awaken joy in me by their joy, some day, maybe even today, I can be joyful enough to awaken joy in others. Or I can call on the 'higher' realms for joy or any other quality, and receive some sort of response to my invocation.

But I think that the discovery that we can communicate and work with all life in the universe on an equal basis gives a special completion and a fresh beginning to our humanity.

My own eternal quest took me as far as I could then go, into the hub of myself and of the universe. From there I was directed to what I thought was a new realm, the angelic world, which in sharing itself kept taking me back to that common hub. From that world I learned more than I could have dreamed about my own pragmatic environment. I learned that we can deal with all levels of our world in a truly creative, reciprocal way and, in joyous company, move to still more creative realms along with the brothers and sisters who make the totality of planetary life.

So far, we have only scratched the surface of the devic world 'within' and 'without' us. We and the universe are full of unknown, changing dimensions, and no space journey could be as interesting or as far-reaching as the journey into our own many mansions. Our angelic brethren, co-builders of our 'inner' and 'outer' universes, show us how to apply our talents in a different way. Just as in the land of Britain I discovered the art of walking, because there people walk, so in the land of the angels I began to discover the art of creative cooperation with my environment.

There is a long journey ahead but, splendidly endowed as we are, we move. And, as the devas said, what matters is that we, the knowing, growing tip of Earth, consciously act from our divine centres.

Appendix

Deva Messages

Fruit Devas *1 February 1964*

*We fruit devas are an especially joyous bunch, we think.
And we produce beautiful, scented blossoms as well as beautiful,
tasty fruit; food especially suited to humans, food good for you
and liked by you. For these reasons, of all our world we should
be closest to you, but it doesn't work out that way. You don't
even recognise us! But we don't mind; we keep happy, because
we could not do our work if we were not happy — and probably
all the fruit would be sour!*

*Happiness is basically important, a secret becoming un-
known to man as he follows his desire for possessions and power.
We wish every human being would listen to us, and understand
that nothing is worth doing unless it is done with joy, that in
any action the radiations of motives other than love and joy
spoil the results, that the end does not justify the means. We
know. We see these things in your actions. You know too, deep
down. Could you imagine a flower being constructed by duty
and then sweetening the hearts of beholders? No, it would not
have the right aura. So we dance through life, creating as we go,
and hope you will join us.*

Rhubarb Deva

We have met before. Whenever anyone contributes atten-
tion or feeling to a plant, part of that person's being mingles
with part of our being, and the one world is fostered. You
humans are therefore all very linked to us, but until you give
recognition to these links, they are as nothing and remain un-
developed. Plants contribute to human food and give of them-
selves in this way, thus building tangible links. Although of the
past, these links can be brought into the present by recalling
them. One great use of memory is to recall the Oneness of life.

Grasses Devas

Not for us to soar in the air conducting magnetic currents!
Munch, munch, munch is heard as we provide food for countless
nibblers on the surface of the Earth, as we keep the soil in place
with our carpet and offer ourselves in leaf and grain. Without
our green covering even sound would be different. We are glad
that so much life depends on us. We are generous, happy servers
and protectors, linking with life below and life that walks the
Earth, life that scuttles and hides — for we are forests to little
folk. We spread and we grow, and we spread again. Without us
it would be a barren, uninteresting world.
Our abundance is general, yet earthbound, creeping to
cover every cranny. We know what we must do and we do it, on
and on. It is well that we don't take umbrage at those who
forever keep cutting us back with teeth! On we go, cheerily,
close to the Earth, close to the rain and the air, on and on. In
this wonderful world we are glad to be alive, glad to grow, just
glad.

Rhododendron Deva

Vivid and sombre, sunshine and rain, and over all a great
love for being, a tenacity and exclusiveness. We settle in wherever

we can, and get down to the business of being. We thank you for bringing us into the garden; we thank all who have allowed us roothold, for we do like to settle.

Each species contributes to and changes the character of the land. Just as your human evolution is moving from functioning as separate individuals or specialised groups, so is the plant world changing, the flora becoming less specialised and more typical of the whole Earth.

Link with us whenever and wherever you see us. This is good for our relationship. Notice us and the way we grow; see us with new eyes. It will help you imbibe our unique quality. The philosophy and the plant life of a country are more related than you might think. Now that greater world unity is possible, let us not lose the essence of each differing contribution. Let us be friends.

Gorse Deva — In the sand dunes   12 June 1967

We surround you with ourselves in the glorious open spaces shunned by others, where we fill the air with our perfume and the hillocks with our gold. Here we bask together. From the innermost realm of pattern, out of air, sand, water and warmth, we cover the waste lands with the perfection of each golden petal. The sun shines on us as our light, our heart, the warmth of our veins, the intelligent giver.

Yes, the angelic hosts enter this dell, where every sound is true and worshipful, where nothing mars or jars. Humans conscious of disharmony through ear, eye or nose are kept at bay, but here with all senses you can turn to your Source. Here the divine link is evident.

To us those links are always clear. We know our oneness with earth, water, heat, air and spirit, in every pore. Humans are blind and distracted, but we are one with the whole, incorporated with that sun. It glows on us; we glow on it.

Whence comes our colour? From the elements we extract and show forth our wisdom, light and shining, warm and complete, yet shy and wild. Could any other colour say as much?

We don light in contrast to the sombreness and tautness necessary to maintain life in these sparse lands. We prove light in our blossom.

Take our essence with you as you go back to your worlds of unreal values. Remember we are whole and complete, that you are whole and complete, and let us always remind you of that.

Aster Deva   *29 August 1967*

Let us share with you again the high delight of the deva kingdom. You humans get so heavy, so filled with concern about one thing or another, that you plummet like a stone to the bottom of a pool; you separate yourselves from us and from the part of yourselves which is one with us. Nevertheless, that part of yourselves is always there beckoning, and it beckons to you on the material level through flowers. Flowers are joy expressed in colour, scent and form, lifting the heart, comforting, speaking of perfection and hope — for if a mere plant can be so beautiful in a sordid world, what can not the human spirit be? We talk to you through our flowers in a universal language, and when you notice us you cannot but respond, for what we have to express you too have to express, and there is perfect harmony between us.

Behind these exquisite forms is a dancing delight of the spirit forever moving free in the perfect rhythms of God, sensitive to the slightest indications from on high, completely attuned to the whole. That too you are, in power, and we would simply remind you of yourselves. Can you not look more in that direction? Look within and you will find that high estate; look without and we will speak of it. Everything will speak of it if your eyes and ears are focused aright. But when you are out of focus, we can still remind you of the wonder of God, we can lift your consciousness.

Yes, we can lift your consciousness; but you, you can lift the consciousness of the planet. We can send out our rays of joy, like little lighthouses; but you, you can move and send your rays of joy to all the world over which you have dominion. We would remind you to do it, and to do it now.

Tibetan Blue Poppy Deva   *16 June 1968*

We carry the aura of our native places, a feeling for the environment most natural to us. Man, taking us from our original home, has spread us all over the world to adorn his gardens. We are pleased with the appreciation, but to remain what we are, it is necessary to keep our links with the places that bred us. Those links you classify as 'shade loving', 'acid soil', etc., but those are the results. It is the 'soul', the overall feel of a place, that influences the direction of growth.

We bring with us the aura of what we are. We who are formless and free can breathe that breath of being into a foreign garden and imbue our plants with their native radiations. Let each garden be different and unique, as is each soul. Man's trend should be to unity, not uniformity. Each to his own talent.

Mock Orange Deva *(Philadelphus)*   *27 May 1968*
(A young, happy-seeming shrub outlined against a neutral wall.)

We are here before you think of us; we are always with our plants. We are attached to each little charge because we love to see it grow and have the keenest delight in being part of its development out of nothing into a perfect example of the pattern we hold. Not one little pore is out of line. Out of the elements we carve and unite, and carve again a living example of one design of the Infinite Designer.

And what fun it is! Each little atom is held in its pattern in joy. We see you humans going greatly about your designs, doing things without zest because 'they have to be done', and we marvel that your sparkling life could be so filtered down and disguised. Life is abundant joy; each little bite of a caterpillar into a leaf is done with more zest than we sometimes feel in you

203

humans — and a caterpillar has not much consciousness. We would love to shake this sluggishness out of man to make you see life as ever brighter, more creative, blooming, waxing and waning, eternal and one.

While talking to you, I am also peacefully promoting growth in the plant. All over the world wherever I grow, I hold the wonderful design for each plant to confirm. Maintaining life in countless places, I yet remain free, utterly and completely free, because I am the life of the Lord. And how I rejoice to be alive! I soar to the highest heaven; I become part of the heart of all. I am here, there and everywhere, and I hold my pattern of perfection without deviation. I bubble with life. I am life. I am one; I am many.

I have leapt lightly into your consciousness. I bow out, glad to have been with you, glad that you have appreciated what I have said, and still more glad to go back to our world of light. Think well of us; think of us with light.

Sweet William Deva   *8 July 1968*

At the time of our blooming you attune to a stationary plant which has an intense radiation of life forces moving in it. You measure both us and yourselves; you list and classify these measurements, separating each characteristic, and yet we are one. All your knowledge, your measurements and your classifications are illusion from the level where we all function as united manifestations of one life. Where we move together, where joy joins us and we speak to one another, there true freedom is, and we move in and out of each other's existence without hindrance.

Do you not see that it is the purpose of life to be fully manifesting on the outer levels, and fully united and conscious of oneness at the same time? That is reality, for your God and my God are one. We scintillate our colours at you, and you scintillate your colours at us, and they are one and the same.

'Unite', we cry. Unite on the face of the Earth and cease, humanity, from despoiling part of yourselves. Have reverence for all that is, for it is part of you and you are part of it.

Love all, for all are forever linked in the One.

Landscape Angel 10 July 1968

*This morning we renew a message. The world is changing;
already the higher vibrations have made a still unrecognised
effect on mankind. The affinity for, and the pull from, the lower
and familiar vibrations are not what they were; this you can see
in the rejection of the young of the orthodox way of life. Everywhere this is happening. What you call tradition no longer has
a deep hold.*

*As always, we see this in terms of forces. The light of the
higher levels now has the magnetic power, which is confusing
because people do not understand its meaning in life. It means
living not for the individual self but for the greater unit, and
mankind has not yet burst the shell of the self. Part of him
knows of this change, part of him cannot reconcile it with
worldly ways. Man is ready to emerge from bondage but does
not know how to do it, does not know where to turn.*

*Now we both know where to turn: to our divinity. Organ-
ised religion says the same, but often does more harm than good
because the force it gives to God is not truly linked with reality.
The noblest and highest human effort, however wonderful —
and it is wonderful — is of no avail unless the glory is given to
the whole. This must be made clear. You are nothing and we are
nothing without those life forces which we are, which are God.
We, the angels, are in a stream of knowing and praising, and all
is well with us in the perfect circle of receiving from God and
giving out again to God. Mankind's destiny is linked with us as
he steps into a new area where he too gives and receives in the
consciousness of the whole. It should be crystal clear that the
glory is God's, that fragmented man in his own strength is nothing. The need of the world is for a conscious turning, to God, to
know that there is one life from One Source.*

We feel it is high time for humans to branch out and include in your horizon the different forms of life which are part of your world. You have been forcing your own creations and vibrations on the world without considering that all things are part of the whole, as you are — placed there by divine plan and purpose. Each plant, each mineral, has its own contribution to make to the whole, as has each soul. Humans should no longer consider us as unintelligent forms of life to be ignored.

The theory of evolution that puts humans at the apex of life on Earth is only correct when viewed from certain angles. It leaves out the fact that God, universal consciousness, is working out the forms of life. For example, according to generally accepted dogma, I am a lowly lily unable to be aware of most things and certainly not able to talk with you. But somehow, somewhere, is the intelligence that made us fair and continues to do so, just as somehow, somewhere, is the intelligence that produced your intricate physical body.

You are not aware of much of your own inner intelligence, and some of your own body is beyond your control. You are conscious of only a certain part of yourself, and likewise you are conscious of only a certain part of the life around you. But you can attune to the greater, within and around you. There are vast ranges of consciousness all stemming from the One, the One who is this consciousness in all of us and whose plan it is that all parts of life become more aware of each other and more united in the great forward movement which is life, all life, becoming greater consciousness.

So consider the lily, consider all that it involves, and let us blend in consciousness, unity and love under the One.

Landscape Angel 14 January 1969

APPRECIATION

We are grateful that you are grateful. Gratitude has an enormous effect, creating a great swelling movement that completes the circle of life. Angels are often shown singing praises, with or without harps, which is one way of presenting the truth that we are always grateful for the wonderful life that is given to us. As we flow with life, as we see the infinite, interlacing, colourful glory of it, the perfection of each aspect, and share in it, we cannot but overflow with thanks and praise to its Source.

In our clear seeing of the flow of life, we complete its cycle by sending back, with full and grateful hearts, the love and light and power given to us. Then the living cycle ebbs and flows. We wish we could convey to you some of the joy, wonder and beauty passing through our beings. Humanity, too, could experience this, but because your consciousness is on another level, you block the flow by not giving thanks. If you could see your life as we do, see the wisdom of each moment, you too would burst into praise, join in the onward movement of the dance, and then see still more to praise. Praise is potent. Try it.

Landscape Angel 18 January 1969

THINKING IN TERMS OF LIGHT

When we ask you to think of plants, or anything, in terms of living light, we are not trying to detract from the beauty of the world seen through human eyes, but to add to that beauty, to add more reality to it, to help you lift all creation. By thinking in terms of light you add light to that already existing; you speed growth and enhance beauty. You see truth and link up with reality.

Man drastically changes the face of the Earth, thinking only that he shifts worthless matter in his levelling of ground and vegetation, or worthwhile (to him) matter in his extracting of minerals, oils, etc. If he thought of everything as living light, as vital substance, he might not alter the landscape so carelessly. For alter he must; his thinking is creative.

Each individual draws to himself the result of his thinking. You think positively about a situation and you manifest a positive result. When you are negative, you draw more negativity to yourself. Therefore it is a practical idea to think in terms of light, and you will get a response from all creation. All creation is light, though obscured by human thought. Even dense matter will respond, and all will be linked in joy. Consciousness will move forward as man links scientifically and inwardly with higher octaves of life. So love the light and change your world.

Good King Henry Deva   *24 May 1970*
(A herb, somewhat like spinach, contacted after I had been reading an old herbal book.)

We come, rather squat and not at all colourful, but with our own virtues — definitely a kitchen plant, and tenacious in our giving.

Remember that we are a result of aeons of history, perfected in the swirls of time and clearly sounding our useful middle note. You read that we are full of iron and good for the blood, and so it may be from your point of view. We have no point of view; we are too busy being and following our pattern to consider what good we are. This is perhaps just as well, or we might become like humans, never content with our lot and always wanting to be as good or better than our neighbour! Comparison seems to us a noxious thing. God made each of us and each of you as we are, to be a particular expression of life.

Yes, I realise that I am comparing, but I see each plant and each human as a compelling rhythm and plan, persistently calling its pattern. In our adherence to our pattern, we wonder why you so often disregard yours. We see the magnificent patterns of light that humans are, and we see them covered and ignored. Devas help to build your patterns for you, and work to keep them pure, while you go your way with your real selves unborn,

208

always there to be but never being. It is very strange.

Know that each plant has a part in the whole and, as a human is the epitome of the whole on Earth, so each plant has a part to play with you. It is good that you all partake of a large variety of plants. Your system can select that which is most helpful at the time. Of course you could choose exactly the right one for you, as the animals do, but few of you take the trouble. If you did, we should probably be more popular!

We continue to sound our unobtrusive note, and are here in case of need. So be it, and all thanks to the Maker of all.

Wild Violet Deva
31 May 1970

(A violet seen in coarse grass in sand dunes, by acres of golden gorse.)

You find in us a power and authority as great as that of the large trees, although we are the smallest flower you have contacted. Yes, this is because we are wild, well-established, free to roam, not dependent on the whims of man. Of course deva patterns are most clearly imprinted where plants can root naturally.

Now come through that outer strength to our distinctive quality. In your mind's eye you see our vivid spots of colour alone among the grasses, visible where the rabbits have eaten the grass. Understand again how related and dependent life is. Oneness is fact, not theory, and all life demonstrates this to seeing eyes.

See also the value of contrast. All around are seas of gorse with millions of blooms, while we are scattered here and there for the sharp eye. The gorse delights with its profusion; we delight with our retiring rarity. You cannot compare us. Each member of Nature is different and unique. But you humans spend your lives comparing what you haven't with what others have, whether it be clothes, gardens, money, views, ailments, time, work, opportunity. All you need is to be what you are, to be the unalloyed pattern of you, and you will draw the right conditions to yourselves. Then your voice will be just as strong,

209

just as right, as any other voice.

You cannot cease wondering at the power of my voice. I have found my niche, I am where God means me to be, and therefore I am as powerful as any in the land. I AM power — I, the synonym for shyness! Nothing in this world or the next can shake those who follow their ordained pattern and do God's will unreservedly. Find and follow God's will for you, and your voice will be power.

It seems that I must begin and end on the note of power — God's power, not mine. But I know you love me for other qualities, and in love I leave you now.

Lavender Deva   *26 July 1970*
(On looking at a lush lavender border with my mind full of problems.)

Rows of us, like the spikes of the plant, seem to be calling you to come, to leave the denseness of human life and join our moving gaiety. Don't you see that all of life can be enjoyed in this spirit? Don't you see that your gloomy view of anything is an unnecessary weight with a reality only in your mind? We know that at birth you are plunged into levels of world thought which are so constantly dinned into you that you accept them as natural and argue that anything else is unrealistic. But now we urge you to look up, rise and accept into your consciousness only that which is good. Accept your problems as something delightful, a game, happy events from which new awarenesses come, for such they are in reality. Let them lift you instead of weighing you down.

There is a way out of your troubles, and it is for you to find it. You won't find it on the level which presents it, where your awareness is confined. Your problem is an opportunity to extend yourself, to let in more light, to rise and enjoy more of life. Someone may point the way, but the problem is one which only your consciousness can solve. You cannot blame anyone else — that is, accurately — and the solution depends on your movement.

210

*We clearly see answers for mankind, just as you clearly see
answers for another, forgetting to apply them to yourself. So
when you find yourself in difficulties, rise and laugh at yourself.
Keep the light touch, which may show you the way. Be grateful
for an opportunity for growth and movement. Don't bemoan
your fate and spread negativity; find and spread light. Life is a
pattern of growth and expansion; move with it and transform
your world. You humans and we angels are of one substance,
and we take every opportunity to emphasise this, to bring a
spark of light to your life, as we do to the life of the plants, and
to join our two worlds in joy. We do love all life very much, as
you will when you rise to yourself. Your attitude is the way; lift
it.*

Soapwort Deva   5 September 1970

*As our scent wafts you to the clear, sparkling air of the
deva world, you realise anew that our shadowless world is the
one you face in the new age. Here everything has its holy place
yet moves to greater strength, for life is positively good, with
nothing to discriminate against or discard. So although we have
not learned discrimination, our mobility and instant action
unites us in a oneness beyond your conception. Each of us, being
fully attuned to the present, individually acts on new energies
while blending with our neighbour.*

*Think of how human affairs would progress if you were
the same! In fact you are the same, and increasingly humans
attune to the present in a greater awareness. Already you notice
this, when you open a book at exactly the right place, when
someone appears at exactly the right time. This instant response
will increase and spread, and your mobility will be as great as
ours. That may sound like nonsense for physical bodies, but
when you are always in the right place at the right time, is that
not perfect mobility? Also, like us, your consciousness need not
be limited by time and space, and will increase its range, experience greater oneness. Oneness has nothing to do with bodies, time,
space or the various mental barriers; love melts barriers.*

211

As you let go the barriers in your thinking, the reality within comes out and oneness appears. Humans have long puzzled us because of the power with which you limit yourselves. Now we rejoice to see barriers tumbling and oneness joining us all. Sound, scent or sight may seem limited to physical levels, but they are equally 'within', part of universal life. So we all move as one, and let us praise life that it is so.

Rue Deva   *5 October 1970*

Do you truly appreciate the wonder of a plant? There is the pattern, held in consciousness by us on what you call the higher levels where energy is particularly clear and powerful, dedicated to the mighty purposes of life of which a planet is the outcome. Then on the lower levels are the results of these different energy patterns: each leaf distinct and beautiful, each flower exquisitely planned and executed, each seed carrying its own life message, each with a flavour, scent and power in some realm of planetary life. Some plants help a wound, some the eyesight, some an emotion, and so on. Is it not a miracle?

It is a miracle of the Oneness of life. You are each intimately related to plants and they to you, and to all creation here on Earth and beyond. In the divine order which sees all things, life is delicately adjusted for its fullest expression on this and other planets, and the whole is affected when the part is out of balance.

But we would emphasise the wonder of life. You, humanity, have your intimations of immortality, and may long for other realms, but perhaps you would focus on and enjoy this life more if you appreciated the ever-present glories and marvels around you, if you appreciated the vast and purposeful concentration of energies making possible the privilege of Earth life. Think of this privilege in terms of time: millions and millions of years have been needed to bring the vehicles of life to their present state of sensitive inter-relationship.

Now that your lack of sensitivity is threatening life, your answer is to be more sensitive, to appreciate the miracle of life

212

and, in your wonder and the love evoked by it, to expand in consciousness. This can be done in scientific terms for those who find wavelengths relevant, but all who see the wonder of life, in a plant or elsewhere, will want to express something of its effect on them. As we are all related, everyone will be relating to each other and to us in their particular art of living.

So appreciate the wonder of life, and expand the planet into its greater destiny.

Godetia Deva   *12 November 1970*

Although in the winter months our plants disappear, the qualities behind are still here. So, if you look at a cheerless grey day and feel your spirits flagging, you can, if you wish, turn to us and become aware of the gaiety of our energy. You can feel the sheer friendliness of it, the irrepressible uplift which is life itself. You can think, if you like, of glowing flower colours, but within is the cause of these in freer form. Within is our world of beauty, calling to every instinct of beauty in you. And strangely enough, beneath even that is still more; a deep peace which broadens to oneness, love, God.

Although our respective outer worlds may be very different, and although our outer worlds may not even be present, within you, human, is the meeting place of all worlds. There we all rejoice together. It is for you to find that place, that all life may be one.

Deva of Christmas Rose   *9 March 1971*

Through the harmful results of his manipulation of life man is proving that planetary life is linked. Some of the damage that he has caused is irreparable, some can be counter-balanced as Nature and man work together. But make no mistake by thinking you humans can leave all the work to us devas; you have to play your part, both in wielding the inner forces towards oneness, harmony and restoration, and outwardly, by ceasing

213

further damage and applying remedies. Man and Nature are both needed in positive cooperation.

Each individual can help in the process. You can spread consciousness of what has to be done, you can use your energies for the whole towards a love of Nature and humanity in a practical way, both inner and outer. You can live according to your knowledge of wholeness, not dwelling on the negative, but pouring healing and love to the whole, remembering that divine forces are at your disposal. Without seeing microbes, without seeing angels, knowing all are part, you can support all manifestations of life. Divine wisdom works sublimely through Nature; it can work as sublimely through you, when you turn to the whole. Only in wholeness can the world be saved.

Landscape Angel   7 May 1971

We call to you, human, from the highest of our realms, and you are there. We call to you from densest earth, and you are there. We call from other worlds across space, and still you are there. We are inwardly still and attuned, and you share our oneness. If there are worlds we cannot reach, no doubt you are there, too. "Man, know thyself."

We talk to you from the kingdom of Nature. Do not limit the wisdom of that kingdom, which is the divine in manifestation and includes obscure worlds which you disregard at your own peril. All around you, in every bit of matter, is what has come from, is, and leads to the only One; and within you is the consciousness that can know and express this. You are all things to all worlds. You incorporate life itself, bound to Earth and bound to Heaven, tiny specks of one small planet in a limitless universe, the image of it all. That is what you are.

But what do you think you are? We know what both we and you are; but you, what do you think? Your thoughts tell you; they are your range of expression and you might just as well let them reflect what you really are. Are they negative or trivial? Then change them, turn them the other way. Use the mighty gift of the pairs of opposites to find oneness, to rise, and

214

turn to what you are. Enjoy what you are; give thanks for it; give thanks to creation and its servers for making you possible. Tune in to what you are; stay put to your immensity. It is for this that we have wielded power through the ages, but now we can know one another and come together for the glory of God. We need call to you no longer; as one we can express wholeness.

Landscape Angel   *19 May 1971*

I would tell you that now, as never before, great Cosmic Angels are reaching to touch Earth in gentleness and beauty. They have done this before, but now the Earth, humanity, has stirred and opened to them. Their touch is wonderful. It may seem to come in the warmth of the sun, it may seem to come in the breeze, it may seem to stretch beyond heaven itself — but it cannot come when you have doubts, fears, burdens or other limitations. When you are yourself master of your conditions, you are one of us. When you are truly yourself, then we can link up with the whole of Earth for you are that Earth.

This is happening increasingly, and, increasingly, the power of our creative gentleness is rising in you. It is not far-off, inapplicable power, but is for your everyday use, for your relationship with all life. It would have no meaning otherwise. It is for all conditions, for the wintry blast as well as the soft spring day; for all is part of the whole, and all has purpose and meaning. You, the Earth, are finding yourself in one universe where all are brothers; and as all become your brothers in your known world, an unknown world opens up in brotherhood. Then all creation sings its song of joy and you hear it, first on Earth and then beyond. You hear that song now, as Nature greets the new day.

Do not doubt the delicate touch of the angels. Glory in it, open to it, and give thanks for it. It is God's hand reaching you from this amazing universe, a consciousness. You were blind, now you see. From space, from all around, unbelievable beauty is coming to you. Open yourself and meet it for it is to be. Praise God.

LOVE

We rejoice that, increasingly, you see the far-reaching effects of love directed to plants. We have stressed, and your religions have stressed, that you love one another; but these words have been just words. The plant world, having no barriers of mind or self to twist what is directed to it, responds immediately. And love is a tremendous power, truly tremendous and sensitive.

It is said that God is love. This is so, and as creation becomes more conscious, it expresses greater love. The essence of life, no matter what its consciousness, is love; and therefore life becomes more perfectly itself when surrounded by love. This is true of all kingdoms, and man's greatest contribution to life on the planet is consciously to love, and so to bring health, vigour and beauty to life.

The gardens of the future will far surpass anything known at present, not because science and intelligence aid or promote them but because love does. The sensitive sharing of love nurtures a plant to its fullness, to its God-essence.

In the coming age, humans will more fully express their God-qualities. As love surrounds them, plants will more quickly express their God-qualities with more openness to change and in greater harmony with the rest of life. Plant miracles will happen, because love is a miracle worker. Plants have been forced and lacerated to bring about certain results; far greater results will be joyfully achieved with love. As you believe in and wield the power of love, you will see this happen.

Another joy that love will bring is a new communion between plants and humans. Just as two humans who love one another have a wonderful rapport, so members of all kingdoms who love have a wonderful rapport.

Now you understand better why we rejoice in your realisation of the power of love. In love's embrace all life becomes more explicitly divine, and God is one in us all.

It is said that there is no perfection on Earth, yet every-where you look you can see it. It is ever changing, moving, from a flower to a dewdrop, from a bird to a sunset, from a taste to a pattern. It is here, depending on how you use your eyes and your other senses, depending on the balance that you have in your physical, emotional and mental bodies. When any of these is so drawn to the particular that it loses its sense of the whole, you are blind. Yet our wholeness, our particular perfect balance, can suddenly come into focus for you and lo, a divine breath pervades your being and all is well. Nothing is said by us. What we are is sufficient, for what we are is what you are: God speaking.

I have a sense of human consciousness saying that God is too mighty to speak through small things. Human consciousness thus seeks to limit God to certain categories, although the atom has proved mighty. Everything, all detail, is important. Every cell and every speck of dust are important and speak in a divine voice. The human task is the ordering and manifesting of a new world; we show you how it is done in our small world, and let our divinity speak to you.